Clarice

a Walk of Faith

Beate H. Keller

Copyright 2018 by Beate H. Keller
The book author retains sole copyright to
her contributions to this book.

Published 2018.
Printed in the United States of America.

All rights reserved. No portion of this book may be reproduced,
stored in a retrieval system, or transmitted in any form or
by any means – electronic, mechanical, photocopy, recording, scanning, or
other – except for brief quotations in critical reviews
or articles, without the prior written permission of the author.

This book is primarily a work of fiction, and the characters
were drawn from the imagination of the author. Any resemblance
to actual people is unintentional.

ISBN 978-1-943650-85-9

Library of Congress Control Number 2018911959

Cover photo by Can Stock Photo/gromovataya.

Published by BookCrafters, Parker, Colorado.
http://bookcrafters.net

This book may be ordered from
online bookstores.

Acknowledgements

Writing this book was a true adventure. If my high school teachers knew that I wrote a book they would feel the need to warn the reader. But my writing was birthed by a calling of God, and to Him belongs all the Glory, and Honor, and Praise.

My gratitude goes towards my family and friends, for all their help and encouragement in writing this book.

My girls, Caroline, Sonja, Elisabeth, Katrina, and Hanna can probably recite the funny and romantic parts of Annette and Roger back to me, after listening to them over and over and over again.

My husband Pat, my son Michael, and my daughter Elisabeth kept the computer going, so I didn't have to confuse my brain with the complicated world of technology.

My dear friends from our writing group, Lynnetta Smith and Penny Storms, encouraged me as I presented bits and pieces of the book, as God gave them to me, for their critique. Thank you for your honesty and encouragement.

Alicia and Robin, thank you for giving me your opinion on the book and for pointing out that the word cattle needed to be substituted with the word kettle. Heather, thank you for taking me to my first Writer's Conference in Glorieta, New Mexico, and for editing my book. Lee, thank you for editing my book and your suggestion, to add another chapter. Nancy, thank you for encouraging me to keep a journal, when God first called me to write. Dee Ann, thank you for taking time to inform me about the world of publishing.

Honorine, Isabelle, and all you prayer warriors, thank you for covering me in your prayers.

My deepest gratitude goes to my Lord and Savior, who called me, equipped me, and guided me every step of the way.

To God, who is above all things, belongs all Glory, Honor and Praise.

Dedication

*I dedicate this book to my grandmother, Hildegard Swoboda,
who lived a life of faith and trust in our Lord Jesus Christ.
And to my husband Pat and our six children.
May you in all challenges of life keep your eyes on
the One who holds you in His hands.*

Prologue

Clarice looked into Quinn's face. He had his arm snug around her and was fast asleep. Clarice's heart was overwhelmed with joy and thankfulness. Everything seemed so hopeless, but God had healed her marriage.

Clarice blinked and turned around. The place next to her was empty. Had she fallen asleep again and did Quinn leave? Or was this just another dream?

Chapter One

I need to tell him how I feel, Clarice thought. *Maybe he will understand.*

That evening, after the children went to bed, Clarice sat across from Quinn. "I need to talk to you."

"What's up?" Quinn reached for her hands.

"You know how I don't like those R-rated movies. I feel like you are mad at me for not watching movies with you. But the sexual content in those movies really hurts my feelings. And when you watch them and look at those naked women, I feel like one of many. It makes me feel like I am not special to you. I share my body only with you and feel hurt when you look at others too."

Quinn sat silently for a moment. Then he said to Clarice, "Honey, my co-worker just lost his job and they are losing their house. My very close friend from high school found out that he has cancer and only six months to live. Our neighbor down the street is getting a divorce. Those are real problems. Don't make something big out of nothing."

Clarice's heart throbbed with pain as she pulled her hands out of Quinn's. Her eyes stung and she left the room. Showing him her tears was the last thing she wanted to do. *He doesn't care,* she thought. *He really doesn't care.* This revelation hit her hard. She knew Quinn to be caring and thoughtful. But it was always on his terms. This hurt more than all those times when he wouldn't answer her questions and made her feel like what she thought and said wasn't important.

Clarice went to bed. She wanted to be asleep before Quinn came in. But sleep wouldn't claim her. She prayed but couldn't get over her hurt. *Am I too sensitive? Is this something every woman has to live with? But Job in the Bible made a covenant with his eyes, to only look at his own wife and no other woman,* she thought.

Clarice pretended to be sleeping when Quinn came to bed. He cuddled up close and tried to pursue her.

"Not tonight," Clarice said, but Quinn didn't give up. She finally left the room and lay down on the sofa.

Quinn followed her. "What's wrong?" he asked with concern.

"Nothing," Clarice lied. *At least nothing you care about,* she thought.

Quinn went back to bed.

The next morning Clarice put on her happy face until everyone left the house. The feelings of hurt hit her hard again when she finally was alone. She allowed her tears to flow unhindered, until there were none left. Tired from the emotional strain, she lay down for a long nap. When she woke up, she felt a little better. There was nothing she could do about Quinn. He wouldn't change for her. Her feelings weren't important to him.

Clarice decided to keep her body hidden from him. She would take showers when she knew he wouldn't see her naked. She would change in the bathroom. She didn't want to be just one of many.

The phone rang and interrupted Clarice's thoughts. "Hello," Clarice said.

"Hi, it's Lydia. You were on my mind, so I decided to call you."

Lydia was one of Clarice's dearest friends. Clarice shared her troubles with her.

"I am sorry, Clarice," Lydia said with compassion. "I don't know what to tell you, except that you can trust God with this problem. He will carry you through."

"I try, Lydia, but I also get discouraged. I feel very hurt. And I am confused. My body aches to be with Quinn, but my heart is hurt. I believe that he is true to me, but sometimes I doubt it, because he also jokes around about other women. He has done this ever since we dated and throughout our marriage. He makes me feel insecure about myself and my body. I often think that he feels he is missing out."

"He wouldn't have married you if he didn't love you. All that talk is probably because he is insecure about himself. Clarice, I would like to continue talking to you, but I have to go. I promise to pray for you and Quinn."

"Thanks, Lydia. I appreciate it. Take care."

"Bye, Clarice."

Clarice hung up the phone. The kids would be home soon and she had to prepare their snacks. She was slicing the last apple when Fiona and Norbert entered the house laughing. "Mom you should have seen this. Paul from down the street was trying to show off on his bike. He did a wheelie and the bike slipped right out from under him and he landed on his behind."

"Was he hurt?" Clarice asked with concern.

"Only his pride," Fiona giggled as she went for her snack.

"How was school?" Clarice inquired.

"Boring." Norbert grimaced as he chewed on his apple.

"We had a pop quiz in math," Fiona sighed.

"Did you do well on the quiz?"

"Of course. But I hate quizzes."

Clarice looked at the clock. "I have to run and pick up Lisa and Isabelle. Please get started on your homework. Dad will be home soon, and we may be able to watch a movie together, if you all get done in time."

"All right," the kids replied as Clarice made her way out the door and to the car.

Lord thank you for my wonderful children. I love them so much and want to bring them up in Your ways. May they grow up to love and follow You.

Clarice arrived at the school and went to Isabelle's classroom. Isabelle had a long face when she exited the room.

"What's up sweetheart?" Clarice asked and embraced her.

"I was picked last for the team in PE. They all laughed."

"Give it some time, Isabelle. When they realize how fast you can run, they will fight to have you on their team."

"Are you sure?" Isabelle asked.

"Absolutely! Let's go and get Lisa."

Isabelle skipped ahead with new optimism.

Lisa came running to Isabelle. "Look, I found a four leaf clover!" she exclaimed as she showed it to her.

"Wow, can you find me one too?"

"I'll look tomorrow." Lisa saw Clarice. "Look Mom, a four leaf clover."

"Great. We'll press it when we get home so you can put it into your collection. Let's go. A snack is waiting for you."

The kids finished their homework in no time with hope for a movie. "Can we make the popcorn for the movie?" Norbert asked.

"Let's eat dinner first. Dad will be here in half an hour. Please set the table."

"That's not my job today."

"I forgot. It's Fiona's turn. Fiona, please come and set the table."

"Can't it wait? I want to finish my book."

"I need for you to do it now."

"I don't want to."

"Please Fiona. I need you to do it now."

"But Dad isn't even here yet."

"Just do it."

"Do it yourself."

"Fiona, if I have to say one more word, you'll be grounded."

"I don't care."

Lord, what should I do? Fiona is totally defiant. I feel helpless. How can I make her understand that she needs to do her part?

Clarice set the table herself. She removed the beautiful bouquet of flowers Quinn had brought her several days ago. When she started placing the napkins, Quinn entered the dining room. "Why are you setting the table?"

"Fiona refused. I told her that she will be grounded if she doesn't do her job."

"Clarice. You have to make the kids do what they need to do. You have to start acting like an adult."

"Quinn, you're unfair. I try my best."

"They don't need a friend. They need a parent."

"I know that. Besides, I don't try to be their friend. I just can't always get them to do what they need to do."

"You need to spank her."

"That's ridiculous. She is already too old for that kind of punishment."

"You don't know anything. You grew up in a small family. This is the way you have to discipline in a large family if you want to see results.

The other kids are watching and will be disobedient if you don't win this one."

"I agree that something has to happen. But you are always too harsh with the kids."

"I am a parent to them. You only want to be their friend."

"I told you that I am not trying to be their friend. But there must be another way to handle their defiance. Maybe we can take some parenting classes together, so we can learn to agree over parenting issues."

"We don't need those classes. I am right. You are wrong."

Dinner was quiet and full of tension. The kids had overheard the fight and ate in silence. Everyone went to bed early.

There was no movie that night.

Chapter Two

One week passed since Clarice had approached Quinn about the R-rated movies. Her thoughts wandered to that day. Quinn's indifference about her feelings tormented her. Other incidences popped into her mind and added to her pain.

The doorbell rang. "Hi, Roger, come on in," Clarice said as she opened the door.

"Hi Clarice. I was in the neighborhood and wanted to see how you were doing."

"Would you like some tea?"

"Tea sounds great."

Clarice filled the water kettle and pulled cups from the cupboard. "Herbal or Earl Grey?" she asked placing the cups on the table.

"Earl Grey would be nice."

Clarice arranged some cookies on a plate and set them next to the cups.

"Are you okay?" Roger asked as he studied her face.

"I could be better," Clarice replied while filling the cups with the hot steaming water.

"What's wrong?" Roger asked when Clarice sat down at the table.

"This might sound weird Roger, but Quinn keeps making jokes about being desired by other women. I understand that we all feel good when we know we are desirable. But when Quinn makes those comments, I feel hurt deep within. To be honest, I want to be the only one in his life and want to be the only one he desires. At times I regret I ever met him. I simply feel unloved by him." Clarice was crying now.

Roger put his arm around her shoulders. He didn't say anything, but his heart broke for his friend. He hated to see her hurt like this. *What a fool Quinn is*, he thought to himself. *How can he make a beautiful woman like Clarice feel so bad? Why didn't I meet her before Quinn?* He thought she was the most beautiful woman there was. How could he help Clarice? She didn't need his assurance, but Quinn's. Life seemed so unfair.

They sat for quite some time. Clarice had laid her head on Roger's shoulder. Finally her tears died down.

"Roger, I'm aware that you can't fix my problem. But I am eternally thankful for your friendship and that I can share my deepest thoughts and hurts with you. I feel like this would be Quinn's place, but unfortunately he doesn't care deeply enough for me to care about my real feelings."

"Why don't you try telling him?"

"I tried," Clarice said with sadness in her eyes. "He made it very clear that my feelings aren't that important to him. Other people have real problems. According to him, mine are small and insignificant."

Roger could have punched Quinn for his cruelty. "Clarice, I don't know if this will help any, but I think Quinn is a fool if he hasn't figured out by now how beautiful and special you are."

"Thank you for your kindness," Clarice said with a weak smile and sipped her tea.

"What are you guys doing this coming Saturday?" Roger asked to divert her thoughts.

"Norbert has a basketball game in the morning, and in the afternoon Fiona has a dance performance."

"Is Quinn going with you?"

"No. He is on a business trip and won't be back until Saturday of next week. I intend to take all the kids to support each other."

"That sounds like fun. Can I come along?"

"Sure. The kids will enjoy spending the day with you. I'll call you Friday night to let you know when to be here. We can all go in my van."

"Sounds great." Roger hugged Clarice. "I have to go now. Hang in there Clarice. I'll talk to you on Friday."

"Bye, Roger."

Chapter Three

Saturday proved to be a wonderful day.

"We have to do this again, Uncle Roger," Isabelle said as she chewed the last bite of her pizza.

"Can we play cards together?" Norbert asked hopefully.

"How about it?" Clarice asked Roger.

"Okay. One game," Roger replied.

"Here are two decks of cards." Fiona handed them to Roger. "Let's play Pick."

Norbert fetched a paper and pen and sat down at the table.

"I want to sit next to Uncle Roger," Lisa declared.

"No, I want Uncle Roger to sit next to me," Isabelle protested.

"Duh," Fiona rolled her eyes, "Uncle Roger could sit between you two."

"How about no more fighting? That way we all can enjoy the rest of the evening," Clarice suggested as she sat down.

"How many cards does everyone get in the first round?" Roger asked.

"Three," Norbert said decidedly. "Isabelle, you are my playing partner. I tell you which card to lay down."

"Okay," Isabelle agreed.

"Who is my playing partner?" Lisa wanted to know.

"I am," Fiona said, who was sitting right next to her.

"It's your turn, Fiona," Norbert remarked.

"I know," Fiona said agitated. "You can lay this card down, Lisa."

"Pick," Norbert declared and won the first round.

When the game was finished, Norbert yelled triumphantly, "Yes! I won!"

"I was so close," Fiona sighed.

"I'll give you lessons," Norbert teased.

Fiona grimaced, "You just got lucky."

"Well that was fun," Roger interrupted their little cat fight. "I have to go now. Thanks for everything."

"I don't want you to go," Isabelle whined.

"We'll see Uncle Roger at church tomorrow, Honey," Clarice declared as she got up from her chair. "Thanks for spending this day with us."

"It was my pleasure. See you tomorrow," Roger replied as he left.

"Okay kiddos. Time for bed," Clarice announced.

"Uhh. Can't we stay up a little longer?" Norbert asked.

"No. Everyone goes to bed. It is very late. I don't want to have you all asleep at church."

"That all depends on who is teaching," Fiona said with a grin on her face.

Clarice only sighed, "To bed everyone." She tucked Lisa and Isabelle in and made sure that Fiona and Norbert turned off their lights. Clarice went to bed tired but happy. It had been a wonderful day.

Chapter Four

"How was the trip?" Clarice asked when she picked up Quinn from the airport.

"It was okay," Quinn replied.

"Did you get the contract settled?" Clarice inquired.

"How are the kids?" Quinn asked, ignoring her question.

Clarice swallowed down her disappointment. "Good," she said sadly.

The rest of the car ride was spent in quiet. Clarice's mind went back to last Saturday. Roger, as always, had been attentive to her and the kids. It was such a wonderful day. Why did there always have to be such tension when Quinn was around? It was like walking on eggshells. Quinn could be super nice and then the next moment be angry and harsh. Clarice sighed. She didn't know how to change it. When they reached the house, Isabelle and Lisa were standing at the window.

"Why aren't they in bed?" Quinn asked gruffly, as they walked to the house.

"They probably couldn't sleep because they wanted to see you."

"Hi Daddy!" the kids said excitedly as Quinn walked in the door.

"Hi. It's time for bed." Quinn said irritated and hung up his jacket.

Isabelle and Lisa went to their room. Fiona and Norbert also disappeared.

He is in a terrible mood, Clarice thought to herself. She tucked the little ones in and checked on Norbert. "Are you still doing homework?" she asked when she found him at the dining room table.

"Yes. I don't understand this word problem," Norbert sighed.

"Maybe Dad can help you."

"Never mind. I'll ask my teacher on Monday," Norbert said as he put his book into his backpack and went to his room.

Clarice knocked on Fiona's door. "Good night, Honey," Clarice said as she peeked into the room.

"Night," Fiona replied.

Clarice went to the living room. Quinn had already turned on the television. "I'm going to bed now," she told him.

No response. Clarice was angry. *Lord, I don't understand Quinn. He does not care to acknowledge me and brings me down with his bad moods. It seems to get worse and I can't stand it.* Clarice fell asleep with anger in her heart.

Chapter Five

Clarice was dropping off Lisa and Isabelle at school when she saw Celestine, a good friend from church.

"How nice to see you, Celestine. I missed you. How was your vacation?" Clarice asked as she approached her.

"It was nice for the most part. I enjoyed getting away from everything for a while. Do you have a little time this morning?"

"Yes. I only have to do some chores at home today."

"I feel terribly embarrassed, Clarice. But I need to talk to someone."

"What's going on Celestine?"

"As I said, I'm really embarrassed about this. I don't know where to start."

"Why don't you come to my house for a cup of coffee? We can talk there."

"Thank you, Clarice."

When they arrived at the house, Clarice brewed a pot of coffee. "Would you like some cookies?" she asked Celestine while she pulled out cups.

"No, thank you. Coffee will be fine." They both sat down at the kitchen table.

"So what is weighing you down?"

"Well, uh um, I don't know how to say this. I, I am having problems with Troy."

"What kind of problems?"

"I feel like he is not listening to me. He complains about everything I do."

Clarice sighed. "I'm sorry to hear that."

"But the worst is that I feel very distant from him. And then there is this guy at work. He listens to me. He encourages me. And he also compliments me a lot. I am drawn to him. Very drawn to him! To be honest, I am falling in love with him. I know it's wrong but I constantly think of him."

"Does he know how you feel?"

"I don't think so. But I have a hunch that he feels the same way about me."

"Has he asked you out?"

"Not really. He is as crazy about dogs as I am and we talked about the dog show next week. He said that he will go and that he hopes to see me there. It's not like a date."

"But he definitely would like to spend more time with you than just at work."

"I think so. Oh Clarice, I can't get him out of my mind. What am I going to do?"

"It's an incredibly hard battle, Celestine. But with God's help it's possible to overcome your feelings for him."

"But how?"

"I know how it worked for me, because I went through something similar. I came to a point where I knew that I'd find myself in an actual affair if nothing changed."

"I had no idea, Clarice."

"Hardly anyone knows that I went through this. The temptation was very strong, but as God promises, He gives us a way out."

"What did you do?"

"I prayed a lot. I cried out to God for help."

"I have done this too."

"It took me a while, Celestine. It was one of my hardest battles."

"But how can you win this battle?"

"You have to keep your eyes on Christ. Spend any time you have in His presence. Continue crying out to God. Read your Bible constantly and claim those scriptures that promise a way out when you're tempted. You can find one of those scriptures in 1 Corinthians 10:13. It says: *'No temptation has seized you except what is common to man. And God is faithful; he will not let you be tempted beyond what you can bear. But when you are tempted, he will also provide a way out so that you can stand up under it.'"*

"It is easier said than done."

"I know it's hard, but you can do it. What God has done for me, by setting me free from the temptation, he can do for you too. I will be praying for you."

"Thank you, Clarice. I am glad I ran into you today. I woke up desperate for help this morning."

"I am glad we got to talk. Call me anytime, and I mean any time, if you need to talk."

"Thanks. I better get going. Today is my day off and I have more than enough to take care of."

"Have a blessed day, Celestine."

"Thanks. Have a blessed day too, Clarice."

Clarice closed the door behind Celestine and went to the kitchen to wash dishes. *Lord I know how hard it is to be faced with that sort of temptation. Please help Celestine through it. Let her be victorious and please help her marriage, too. Help Troy to accept You as Lord and Savior. I don't want their marriage to fall apart. It is incredibly hard to be unevenly yoked. But I believe that You can reach Troy.* A tear ran down Clarice's cheek. *And please reach out to Quinn, too.*

Chapter Six

"Mom, oh Mom," Isabelle said with tears in her eyes. "The booklet about the planets is due tomorrow and I haven't even started."

"When did you know about the assignment?"

"Since Thursday before Spring Break."

"Oh, Honey. You had this whole week to work on it."

"I know. But I forgot. Now I will get an 'F' and end up with a 'D' in this class," Isabelle stuttered through her tears.

Clarice took her into her arms. "It is already close to bed time, but I'll give you a little time to work on the booklet. Maybe you can still finish. I will type it for you in the morning."

"Thank you, Mom."

"I can help too," Lisa tried to encourage her younger sister. Together they sat at the computer and Lisa showed Isabelle how to find the information about the planets. Then Lisa went back to her chores while Isabelle worked on her project.

Clarice had been up since early morning and her energy had worn off. "I have to go and rest, so I can get up early to type."

"Thank you, Mom. And I am sorry I forgot."

"It's okay, Honey. We all forget at times. I love you." Clarice kissed her forehead.

"I love you too, Mom."

Lisa had already made her way to bed. Clarice went to her room and kissed her good night.

"Can you sing to me?" Lisa asked.

"Of course," Clarice smiled at her and sang Lisa's special lullaby.

"Thank you, Mom."

"You're welcome. I love you. Have sweet dreams."

"I love you, too."

Clarice prepared for bed. *Thank you for this wonderful day*, she prayed. *It's always good to see my friends at church and to spend time with the children baking and playing. I feel terrible that Isabelle is up late but hopefully she can finish her project. Be also with Fiona and Norbert at their sleepover and protect them.* Clarice had allowed them to spend the night at a friend's house since middle school was off the next day.

Clarice lay down and fell asleep only moments later. She woke up early the next morning. After getting ready for the day, she sat down with a cup of tea and her Bible.

Please open my mind, Holy Spirit, that I may understand what I read, she prayed. When she was finished reading she went to her favorite Bible verses, which she claimed for Quinn, the kids and herself. *"May the Lord our God be with Quinn, the children and me, as He was with our fathers. May He never leave us nor forsake us. And let our hearts be fully committed to You oh Lord, to live by Your decrees and obey Your commands.* (1 King 8: 57&61) *Please form our hearts in a way* (Psalm 33:15) *that we may love You with all our heart, soul and mind* (Matthew 22:37) *and that we may follow You wholeheartedly* (Deuteronomy 1:36). *Let us be completely humble and gentle, let us be patient, dealing with one another in love (Ephesians 4, 2). Let us be kind and compassionate to one another, forgiving each other, just as in Christ God forgave us* (Ephesians 4:32).

Clarice took a sip of her tea and continued praying. *Thank you, Lord, for Your scriptures and that I can claim them for my family. Be also with my extended family and my dear friends and bless them. Be especially with Celestine and help her to stay strong in You. I love You, Jesus. Father, I love You. Holy Spirit, I love You and thank you for being my helper as the Bible promises.*

Clarice put her Bible aside and went to the computer. Isabelle had done a fine job finding facts and Clarice typed them into the computer. When she was finished she went to wake Isabelle. "Honey, it's time to finish up your project."

Isabelle was sound asleep. "Come on, Isabelle. You have to get up. It's time. Hey there, get up."

"I'm so tired Mom," Isabelle managed to say softly.

"I know, but you have to get up, Honey. You still have to put the booklet together. I typed it for you."

"Oh, Mom. I typed it myself already. Sorry about that."

Clarice sighed, "It's okay. But you still have to put it together."

Isabelle sat up in bed. "I didn't get to finish it. I fell asleep at 1 a.m."

"You were up till when?" Clarice asked as her stomach turned.

"Till 1 a.m. Then I fell asleep."

"Oh my. I didn't mean for you to stay up that late. This day will be rather hard."

"I know and I only finished half the work."

"Well, Honey, let's put together what you have and then hand it in today. Explain to the teacher that you forgot the assignment and that you will finish it later, even if you will receive no credit."

"Yes, Mom. And I'm sorry you got up early to type."

"That's okay, Honey. I just wish you would have finished the facts instead, so I could have helped. Get ready and meanwhile I'll make you a power breakfast to help you stay awake."

"Thank you, Mom."

Oh Lord, Clarice prayed in her heart. *I feel awful that Isabelle stayed up that late. She'll have a horrible day. I should have sent her to bed instead and have her go to school without her project. But she was so upset about receiving an 'F'.*

"Breakfast is ready, Isabelle," Clarice said as she turned around. But Isabelle was on the sofa, sound asleep again.

"Come on, Honey. You have to eat."

"I feel like throwing up, and my head is pounding."

Clarice stroked her head. *She'll sleep through her classes*, Clarice thought to herself. "Go back to bed, Isabelle," Clarice told her.

"Thanks, Mom," Isabelle mumbled and dragged herself back to bed.

What a mess, Clarice thought. *Isabelle's efforts were in vain and she will miss school on top of it. Why didn't I give her a time limit? But I didn't expect her project to be so complex.*

Lisa came into the kitchen. "Mom, I'm late. Can you take me to school please?"

"Yes. Eat while I'm changing my shoes."

Lisa took a pancake and some eggs. She stuffed the last piece of egg into her mouth when Clarice came back to the kitchen. "Let's go," Clarice said and grabbed her purse.

Clarice dropped Lisa off and made her way to Giuseppe's, her favorite restaurant. She took a seat and ordered two cups of tea.

"Hi, Clarice," Lydia said as she took her place across from Clarice. "Have you waited long?"

"I actually just arrived a few minutes ago. I ordered a tea for you. What did the doctor say?" Clarice asked.

"He said I need to do stretching exercises. I was worried that I might need surgery."

"That's good news! I was concerned for you."

"Thank you, Clarice," Lydia said as she studied Clarice's face. "Are you all right, Clarice?"

"Why do you ask?"

"Something is going on. I can see it in your face. Want to talk about it?"

"Okay. Actually, I feel totally unfit as a mother to my children."

"Why do you say that?"

Clarice explained the whole dilemma with the project and how Isabelle wasn't able to go to school. "Why can't I be wiser? I always make those horrible mistakes. To be honest, I wish my kids had a mom who had it more together."

"Clarice, don't be so hard on yourself. You made a wrong choice. But it was out of love. We all miss it at times."

"Yes. But I miss it so often."

"You weren't made to be perfect. It is not hard to see that you love your children very much. And they know it too. You keep looking at what you do wrong. But you do right far more than wrong."

"I hope so, but I feel totally condemned."

"Clarice, God covers your shortcomings with His love. He also promises that 'All things work together for good to them that love God.' I know that you love God, Clarice. Besides, God in His great care has chosen you to be their mom. Trust God. He doesn't make mistakes."

"I can't argue with that. But I still feel bad when I mess up."

"We all do. Believe me though, that your love outweighs your mistakes."

"Thank you for your encouragement."

"I'll pray for you and Isabelle when I do my stretching exercises after lunch."

"Thanks. What kind of stretching exercises are you supposed to do?"

"The doctor gave me this sheet of ideas to get started. I don't like to exercise, but if it relieves the pain, I'm more than willing to do it."

Clarice looked at the paper, "Actually this looks like fun. Maybe I can join you and do those stretching exercises together with you."

"That would be great. How about tomorrow?"

"Tomorrow I have an appointment. Thursday would be better."

"It's a deal. Just meet me at my house," Lydia said.

"I'll do that. It's already 9:30 a.m. I have to go."

"Me, too. I have 1001 things to do today."

"Good luck with everything. Bye, Lydia."

"Bye, Clarice."

Clarice left the restaurant and ran errands. When she was finished, she picked up eggs and milk and headed for home.

Isabelle was sitting at the dining room table doing her homework. "Guess what," Isabelle said. "My friend just called and told me that the booklet wasn't due today. It is due in two weeks. But I am almost done. Look," Isabelle said as she held up her work.

"I am glad to hear that. The booklet looks great so far."

"Thanks. I also will be able to finish my homework for tomorrow. Natasha told me the assignments."

"Great. I better let you get back to work."

"What's for dinner tonight?"

"Chicken pot pie."

"Yum."

"I have to hurry. There was a big accident on the highway today and I lost a lot of time. Did Michelle's mom drop off Lisa?"

"Yes."

"Where is Lisa now?"

"She is in her room studying her spelling words."

Clarice stepped into Lisa's room. "How is it going with the spelling?"

"Pretty good, Mom. There are only two more words I need to work on."

"Do you want me to give you a practice test?"

"Yes."

Clarice practiced the list with Lisa and went back to the dining room. Where are Fiona and Norbert?" she asked Isabelle.

"I don't know," Isabelle replied.

Clarice went to their rooms and found them both sleeping. She went back to the kitchen and began to prepare dinner. She was almost done when Quinn came home. He came up behind Clarice, embraced her, and gently placed a kiss on her neck. "What's for dinner?" he asked.

"Chicken pot pie," Clarice announced, leaning into him.

"Great. I am starving," Quinn said.

"It will be done in about ten minutes."

"Where are the kids?"

"Isabelle is in the dining room doing her homework, Lisa is in her room practicing spelling, and the other two are fast asleep in their beds."

"Why are they sleeping?"

"I guess they were up all night with their friends at the sleepover."

"I'll wake them."

"I think we should let them sleep. They will be grumpy."

"No, we eat together."

"I think we should make an exception today."

"You make too many exceptions all the time."

"That's not true. I just think that there will be unnecessary conflict if we wake them."

"I'll wake them."

Oh God, I see trouble coming. Please help me to know what to do, Clarice prayed. "Isabelle, please tell Lisa to set the table."

"Okay, Mom," Isabelle replied and went to her sister's room.

Clarice heard arguing from Fiona's room. She rushed to the room and saw Quinn dragging Fiona out of her bed, crying. "Please, Quinn. Let her be."

"No, Clarice. She will sit at the table with us. Go away. Let an adult handle this situation."

Quinn's words stung her heart. Clarice felt helpless and defeated. Was she wrong? There must be a better way to deal with this situation, but she couldn't think of anything.

Finally everyone was gathered around the table. Clarice forced down some food, while Fiona and Norbert just sat there, angry. Lisa and Isabelle ate in silence. A heaviness lay in the air.

Quinn had gotten his way, but at what cost?

Chapter Seven

Clarice reached for her phone, "Lydia, this is Clarice. Can I come over for a little while?"

"Of course. I don't have anything planned this afternoon."

"I'll be there in about ten minutes," Clarice said. She gathered her purse and car keys and was on her way. Lydia had a pot of hot tea ready when Clarice arrived. Both sat down at the kitchen table.

"So what's on your mind?" Lydia asked while pouring tea into their tea cups.

"Oh, Lydia," Clarice began, "I don't know what to do. Fiona and Norbert are giving me such a hard time. They have started to be very disrespectful to me."

"Have you talked to Quinn about it?"

"I have tried in the past. But his answer is to spank them, and I don't believe this is the right way to discipline teenagers."

"I agree with you. You will have to figure out other consequences."

"I know. But I feel helpless. I have prayed for wisdom but God doesn't seem to answer. When I give the children consequences for wrong behavior, I feel guilty because I feel I was too severe, and then I don't follow through."

"It is a little hard for me to advise you Clarice, since I don't have any children of my own. But I heard that it is important to not go back on your word."

"I know. I try to take my time to think about consequences that are fitting before I make them known. But to be honest, most of the time I can't come up with anything. I feel so totally lost. I wish I could talk to Quinn and figure out a way to deal with this problem. But where I am too lenient, he is too strict. When Quinn is around I don't address the issues at all, because when he hears the kids argue with me and being disrespectful, he punishes them in a way that doesn't seem right. But I know that something has to happen. I feel so helpless and lost. I don't know what to do. I don't know where to find help."

Lydia put her hand on Clarice's shoulder, "I am sorry that you have to deal with all this. It seems to me that you and Quinn might need counseling."

"I suggested it to him, but he keeps saying we don't need counseling, and I just need to act like an adult."

Lydia put her hand on Clarice's in shock. "He said that to you?"

"Yes and worst of all, he says these kinds of things in front of the children."

"Clarice, I really think that counseling has to happen. If Quinn treats you in this way, the kids will get worse in their disrespect toward you."

"Maybe Quinn is right. I mean, often I don't know how to discipline the children and, as an adult, I *should* know what to do."

"It is a fact that adults don't have the answers for everything. And it just so happens that you struggle with disciplining. But that doesn't give Quinn the right to belittle you in that way."

"I don't know Lydia. Besides, I really wish the children had a better mom."

"Clarice, I told you before and I'll tell you again, God has chosen you as their mom for a purpose. He knows what He is doing."

"But why doesn't God answer my prayers and give me wisdom on how to discipline the children? I have prayed so hard and don't feel any guidance at all."

"I know that it is hard when we feel our requests are being unanswered. But don't give up praying and believing. Satan would love to see you fall away."

"You don't have to worry about me losing my faith. God is all I truly have. Even if He doesn't answer me, I won't be able to turn away from Him. Quinn has tried to separate me from the Lord without success, and believe me, it is hard. Often he tells me I can't go to church because the house isn't in order. But I won't let him take church and Christ away from me, no matter how much I suffer because of it."

"I am glad to hear that you stay strong in the Lord, Clarice. God won't disappoint you."

"I just wish Quinn would understand my convictions and wouldn't fight so much against what is so dear to my heart. The children are caught in the middle of this battle. Sometimes they fight me on going to church. But I insist that they come with me. I can't make them accept Jesus as their Lord and Savior. But I will expose them to the truth whenever I can."

"I would do the same if I had children. As it says in scripture, *'How can they believe in the One of whom they have not heard.'*"

"Where can I find that verse? I would like to read it in its context."

"It's in Romans 10:14. I have it memorized because I thought it is so profound."

"I will try to memorize it too. It is amazing to me, to see the deep meaning of the words in the Bible. Since Christ has gotten ahold of my heart and I made a commitment to follow Him, there are days when I read the Word for hours."

"I also get lost in time when I read the Bible. Do you read the Bible together with the children?"

"Sometimes yes. But often I am too tired," Clarice sighed. "Talking about the kids, I need to pick them up from school in a few minutes. Thanks for lending me your ear."

"I am always here for you, if you need me. You know that."

"Thanks Lydia. I'll see you at church on Sunday."

"Bye, Clarice."

Chapter Eight

Clarice felt numb as she read the e-mail again. At first she couldn't feel anything but heaviness. Why was Quinn so mean? How could he write in a way so judgmental and degrading about his wife and his children? It nearly broke Clarice's heart. Clarice wasn't surprised about the meanness of the words. She had read similar summaries of her family before. But she was never prepared for her feelings being hurt so deeply. Why did she still hold on to this man? Was there any hope for her marriage and family?

The phone rang. "Hello," Clarice tried to control her shaky voice.

"Hi Clarice, it's Lydia. I just received an e-mail from Quinn."

"I just read it too," Clarice's voice broke and she started to cry.

"I am so sorry," Lydia said. "Are you home?"

"Yes," Clarice sobbed.

"I'll be over in a few minutes." Before Clarice could say anything, Lydia hung up the phone, grabbed her jacket and purse and drove over to Clarice's house. Clarice was washing her face when the doorbell rang.

"Thank you for coming over. I just don't know what to do anymore," Clarice whispered while tears started rolling down her face again. Lydia embraced her.

Oh Lord, help my friend and fill her with peace, Lydia prayed in her heart, still standing and embracing Clarice. After a while Clarice calmed down and Lydia led her to the sofa in the living room.

"I don't understand why Quinn is so hateful, and why he puts us down in this way. He tells everyone that I talk to God and that God can't make up His mind what I should do. Quinn doesn't understand that God is the very

One who encourages me to hold on to His promise of a healed marriage and family. If it wasn't for God, I would have left Quinn years ago. And now I am about ready to give up and divorce him. I just don't see any hope anymore. My heart feels like a raw wound."

Lydia put her hand on Clarice's shoulder. "You remember the story about the single foot prints in the sand? God is carrying you right now. He knows your deep hurt."

"I know," Clarice said with a bleak voice. "But I still feel numb and hurt at the same time. I wish God would take me home right now. Life is way too hard and I desire to be in His loving arms away from all this."

"Now listen Clarice, God still has a great plan for your life. You can't simply just give up."

"I know," Clarice sighed. "But from time to time the burden gets too heavy."

"Then give that burden to Jesus. He already carried it on the cross."

"I know, Lydia, I know." Clarice stared at the carpet. A few minutes passed.

"I promise to pray for you, Clarice," Lydia said.

"Thank you, Lydia. God's my only hope," Clarice said. A moment later she looked up at Lydia. "Some kind of hostess I am. I didn't even ask if you would like something to drink. What would you like?"

"Don't worry about that right now," Lydia said but Clarice had already made her way to the kitchen to get hot water going. Lydia followed her.

When they sat down at the table to drink their tea, Lydia asked, "Where are the kids?"

"They are still at school." Clarice took a sip of her tea and looked at the clock at the kitchen wall. "Oops, it's already time to pick them up. Would you like to come along?"

"Actually I can't. I have to go and get ready. Tom will be home early to take me out for dinner and a movie."

"I forgot. It's your anniversary today. And I burdened you with all my problems."

"Don't worry about it. I am glad that I was able to come."

"Me, too. Say hi to Tom and enjoy the evening."

"I will. See you later."

Chapter Nine

A month had passed and the tension had reached an intensity that left Clarice desperate. *Lord, I can't handle this anymore,* she cried, *I have tried so hard, but everything is falling apart. Quinn is not only hurting me but also the children with his degrading comments. I don't understand why he is so harsh to us, but I can't tolerate his behavior anymore. Putting me down and spreading lies about me is one thing. I don't measure myself by him; even so, it cuts deep into my heart. But doing this to the kids is inexcusable. I can't allow it any longer. I know that you hate divorce but I simply can't bear it anymore. I don't want my marriage to end. Maybe separating from Quinn will help. It hurts to do it, but this craziness has to stop.*

Clarice got up and went through the house, collecting Quinn's things. Today he would be home much earlier than the children so they would be spared the fight. She filled two suitcases with his stuff and put them on the porch.

When Quinn arrived home, he had a puzzled look on his face. "Who is going on vacation?" he asked, as he shifted the chocolates he had bought for Clarice in his hands.

"Nobody," Clarice replied. "These are your things."

"What do you think you are doing?" he asked, suppressing the anger and insecurity he felt inside.

"It's over, Quinn," Clarice said with tears in her eyes. "I need you to leave."

"Don't be rash. We can work this out, whatever it is."

"I am not rash. I've told you over and over that our marriage is falling apart, but as usual, you disregarded my feelings. And now it is too late."

"But I love you, Clarice."

"Don't get me wrong, Quinn. I love you too and will always love you. But I can't live like this anymore."

"I have given you everything. You have freedom with the finances. You have a car. I bring you flowers. No other husband would ever be that good to you."

"I know you have so many good qualities and I will greatly miss them. But I can't live with that dark cloud over us anymore."

"What do you mean dark cloud?" Quinn snapped at her.

"I simply never know from one moment to the next if things will be okay. Your moods change without warning, and I walk on eggshells. You hurt us with your words and don't even know it. This is not good for any of us, especially the kids."

"If you would have a better handle on Norbert and Fiona things would be different. It's your fault that we're in this dilemma."

"I know that I need help guiding Norbert and Fiona into the right direction. I feel incompetent at times and would welcome your aid. But you only add to the problem instead of helping me. I wish we would have gone to classes together that would have assisted us in finding a way together to deal with the kids and…"

"I told you over and over that my way is the right way. You are just acting like a child."

"Stop this and leave. I want to be left alone. Go or I'll call my friend."

"You are a weakling. Always asking others for aid. Always asking God for help. How pathetic."

Clarice picked up the phone and started dialing.

"Oh forget it," Quinn threw the chocolates to the floor. "You will see the day when you'll regret sending me away." He slammed the door as he left.

Clarice's hands shook as she put the phone down. She sank onto the sofa and started sobbing uncontrollably. Hours had passed when Clarice heard the door. She dragged herself to the bathroom and washed her face. It was red and swollen from all the crying.

"Where is Dad?" Norbert and Fiona asked when they entered the house. "He said he'd be home early today."

"What's wrong?" Fiona asked when she saw Clarice's face.

"I broke up with Dad."

"Finally," Norbert said under his breath.

Fiona took her things and locked herself into her room.

This was going to be harder than Clarice had foreseen. Right now she was too exhausted to deal with the aftermath of the separation.

Lisa and Isabelle came home late. They had gone to the movies with a friend and her mom. When Clarice opened the door, the girls started talking at the same time.

"That was the best movie ever. Mickey Mouse was so cute."

"Isabelle has a crush on a cartoon character," Lisa teased.

"No I don't."

"The popcorn was delicious with lots of butter."

"Ivey's Mom also bought us candy and soda."

"What's for dinner?" Isabelle asked.

"I'm full," Lisa groaned.

Clarice tried to take everything in, but felt overwhelmed.

"Where is Dad?" Lisa asked. "I want to tell him that Isabelle has a crush on Mickey Mouse."

"Please sit down you two. I have to tell you something."

"But I am hungry Mom," Isabelle protested.

"This is important."

Both girls sat down and looked at Clarice with anticipation.

"I have decided to separate from Dad."

"You mean divorce?" Lisa asked.

"No. But we need some time apart from each other."

"Will we ever see him again?"

"Yes, any time you want to."

"Why, Mom?"

"I can't explain it to you. I know that this is hard for you, but I needed the change. Please wash up. Dinner will be ready in a few minutes."

"I'm not hungry anymore," Isabelle whispered sadly and went to her room.

"I want to go to bed now," Lisa yelled and went to her room.

Clarice felt terrible. This was a no-win situation. She felt terribly hopeless.

Chapter Ten

A month had passed since the separation. Clarice was folding clothes when the phone rang. "Hello," Clarice said.

"Hi, it's Lydia. We are back in town."

"It's good to hear your voice. How was your vacation?"

"Fantastic. Tom didn't tell me what he had planned for us until we parked in front of a small Bed and Breakfast deep in the woods. It was beautiful there. I didn't want to come back home. We even got to do some horseback riding."

"Where did you find horses so deep in the woods?"

"We drove to the edge of the woods where a family has a farm with horses. The owners were so nice. We rented two horses for the day and followed a trail through the woods that led us to a clearing where we were able to give the horses full rein. It was so much fun."

"Do you have any pictures?"

"Yes. Why don't we meet at Giuseppe's? That way you can see the photos we took."

"Sounds great. How about in half an hour?"

"Okay. See you there."

Clarice hurriedly finished the laundry and went to Giuseppe's. Lydia already sat in their favorite spot and waved to Clarice.

"My, it is good to see you." Clarice said as they embraced. "I missed you a bunch."

"I missed you too. Sit down here," Lydia said tapping the chair next to her. "That way we can look at the pictures at the same time."

The waiter came and both ordered a tall glass of lemonade.

"This one looks totally goofy," Clarice laughed pointing at one of the pictures. "What were you guys doing?"

"We pretended to be Outer Space tree-huggers."

"You two are the perfect fit. Serious when it is called for and funny all the rest of the time."

"I guess I have to agree."

"You took quite a lot of pictures," Clarice said looking at some of the last photographs.

"These are only the pictures we kept. You should have seen how many we deleted until it boiled down to this collection."

"I think this is my favorite. You both look so totally in love leaning against each other on that rustic bench."

"I like it the best, too. Tom makes me feel complete. I love him so much."

"I am very happy for you, Lydia."

Lydia saw the sincerity in Clarice's eyes but also a hint of pain. "I wish it was the same for you and Quinn," she said compassionately.

"Me too," Clarice sighed. She drank some of her lemonade. "Separating from Quinn wasn't easy. I miss him a lot. But at least the horrible tension in the house is gone. Quinn continues to write hurtful e-mails about the kids and me and sends them to everyone. I don't read his e-mails anymore but the kids do. It hurts them deeply. I know that none of us are perfect. But I don't understand why Quinn is constantly looking for something bad about us to share with the world."

"I stopped reading Quinn's e-mails, too. Tom shares with me from time to time what Quinn is writing. We almost decided to block his mail from our account. But Tom decided that we can use these e-mails to pray for Quinn more specifically. The e-mails reveal quite a lot about Quinn. I think that God has to get ahold of him for anything to change."

"I agree. That is my only hope." Clarice seemed to be far away in her thoughts. Lydia prayed silently for her friend while waiting patiently for Clarice to sort her thoughts.

After a while Clarice picked up her favorite photo of Lydia and Tom again. "I am so glad to know you and Tom," she said. "Your marriage encourages me."

"I believe that God will heal your marriage, Clarice. And He will bless you for waiting on Him."

"Thanks Lydia. I feel deep down in my heart that God will do so. It is just hard to wait."

"I know. So how are things going with the children?"

"About the same. We have some very good times which I enjoy to the fullest. But when it is bad, it is really bad. I don't understand how the kids can be so mean and disrespectful. I try my very best, but I often feel like I'm a total failure."

"Don't feel too discouraged. There are many parents out there who deal with difficult teenagers. It doesn't mean that you are failing. Just keep praying for your children and one of these days you will see how God answered your prayers in their lives."

"I am thankful that I have such a wonderful God. Without Him I couldn't do it."

"I feel the same way." Lydia said. She quickly looked at her watch. "I have to leave now. Thanks for coming to see the pictures."

"Thanks for sharing them with me. They are beautiful. Will you be at church this Sunday?"

"Yes. Tom is off from work so we both can go together."

"I'm looking forward to seeing you two lovebirds there. Say hi to Tom for me."

"And you say hi to the kids."

"I will," Clarice said and hugged Lydia good-bye.

Chapter Eleven

"It hurts so bad," Clarice said as she pulled out a tissue. "I'm sorry to always burden you with my problems."

Clarice had called Roger at least a dozen times since her break-up with Quinn and he had always lent her an ear. Today Roger had come over and now sat down beside Clarice. He put his hand on her shoulder and said, "You should know that you are no burden to me. I really care for you. You are one of my very best friends." *If you weren't married to Quinn I would like to become more than a friend to you*, he thought to himself. But he knew better than to voice that thought to her.

Clarice sat up straight and wiped the rest of her tears away. "Everything would be so much easier if I didn't love Quinn. But he still means so much to me. Why doesn't he understand? I can't live like this." Tears threatened to come up again. What if it was indeed over? What if Quinn would divorce her? Her hopes for a healed marriage had been so high. But she knew she couldn't change Quinn. He didn't understand her relationship with Jesus and that was their biggest problem. Quinn lived worldly and Clarice's greatest desire was to follow God and bring Him joy. But what about the children? They suffered from the separation and would suffer even more in the event of a divorce. But there was no way to live together the way it had been. The children had endured enough. If Quinn didn't turn to the Lord the family would stay broken, even if they were reunited.

Clarice's pain was indescribable. Her insides still felt like an open wound. But she also remembered that she was unhappy and hurting before they separated. Her only hope was in the Lord. But what was His will? Did He want to heal this marriage and family or did He want to give Clarice and the children a new start? Clarice couldn't picture herself ever marrying again. She still loved Quinn. Besides, she felt like she was failing this marriage to Quinn already. How could she expect to have a successful marriage with a new partner? Wouldn't she just bring the hurt from her first marriage into the next?

Roger was sitting there waiting for Clarice to feel better. Clarice's thoughts came back to Roger. "I am sorry. Here you are right beside me and I spend time in my own world."

Roger looked at her. "You don't have to be sorry. It must be hard for you to be in this situation."

Clarice looked into Roger's eyes. The tenderness and love she saw caught her by surprise. This was not the way a friend looks at another friend. Clarice looked away. No, Roger was her friend and nothing more. But didn't she always feel accepted and loved when she was around him? Was there more between them than a friendship? Clarice got up. "Would you like some tea?" she asked.

"Actually a glass of water would be nice," Roger answered.

Clarice went into the kitchen. She pulled out the orange juice and filled a glass. *This simply can't be true,* she thought to herself. *He is my friend and that's it.* She took the glass of juice to Roger who chuckled: "I didn't realize that you have colored water."

Clarice looked at him puzzled. "Didn't you ask for juice?" she asked.

"Actually no. But juice sounds good, too." He took the glass from her hand and had a sip. "That's mighty good orange juice. I bet Isabelle made you buy it."

"I know I need to buy some apple juice," Clarice said.

Roger was confused about her answer but chose to stay quiet. Obviously something was bothering Clarice and her thoughts were miles away. He finished his juice quickly saying, "I think it is time for me to go. Call me when you need me. And say hi to the kids."

Clarice sat down at the kitchen table. She was thoroughly confused. What just happened? She sat for quite some time. The phone rang, but she let it go. When the answering machine kicked in she heard Lisa's voice: "Mom, aren't you picking us up? We are at the ..."

Clarice ran to the phone and picked it up. "I'm on my way," she said and rushed to the door. "Oh no! My purse," she mumbled as she ran back into the house.

Fortunately the school was close by. When she drove up, Lisa and Isabelle ran to the car. "Hi Mom," the girls yelled cheerfully.

"Hi, you two. Sorry that I am so late," Clarice replied.

"That's okay," Lisa said. "We chatted with the nurse and you know how much she enjoys that. Tomorrow …" Clarice tried to concentrate on her children but her thoughts always came back to Roger. She started to feel drawn to him. No, she thought to herself. *I can't allow myself to think about him. I am married. Besides I probably saw things that aren't true.*

When they arrived at home the girls were quiet. "What's wrong?" Clarice asked.

"Nothing," Isabelle said. "Except that you haven't answered our questions."

"Oh, I am sorry," Clarice said and turned to the girls. "What did you need to know?"

"Tomorrow is a special party at school and we volunteered to bring cookies."

"That sounds fine. You can make two batches. That way we can have some too."

The girls ran into the kitchen.

"Haven't you forgotten something?" Clarice asked.

The girls looked at her. Clarice pointed to the backpacks and the jackets they had thrown on the floor. "Oh, sorry, Mom," they said and put their things away.

Clarice concentrated on the baking and was occupied with cooking, homework and laundry for the rest of the day. When night came she fell into bed. Her thoughts returned to Roger. He was a really good friend and the children liked him a lot.

Was he perhaps to be her husband? But no, she was still married. She couldn't allow herself to think about another man. If he were to be her future husband then God would keep Roger available for her. As for right now, she was married and committed to Quinn. God could still heal this marriage. He is the Almighty One. And He has the best plan. It would be the very best, especially for the children, if this marriage would be healed.

Clarice rolled over in her bed. She had to make a choice: She could dwell on Roger and imagine what life with him would be like, or daydream how her life with Quinn could change and be restored. Clarice chose to pray for Quinn. He needed God in his life. *Oh Lord, let Quinn know how much he needs You. You want to be his Lord and Savior. This is the only chance for our marriage to be restored. We all need more of You and need to be transformed by Your love. I know that there are areas in my life that have to change. Please come and heal my heart. Fill me with Your Holy Spirit yet again. I want to bring You joy, praise, and glory with my life. And I desire for my family to be healed.* With those thoughts she fell asleep.

Chapter Twelve

Clarice's hands were sweating. How would Quinn react? She was afraid of the rejection that she had felt so often. There he was. She still felt very attracted to him. She desired no other man, but the physical aspect was not enough for their relationship.

Lord, how can he understand the hurt I feel when he ignores me and when he puts me down? As a wife I should desire to be loved. But I also feel such a need to be respected for who I am. He treats me like I am inferior. I feel like he never really cared for my feelings, never took my warnings seriously, that our marriage was in trouble and that we needed help, until I finally sent him away. But that very act brought him so much pain. I never wanted to hurt him. Oh Lord, what can we do? Is our marriage going to end up in divorce? I want it so much to be restored. But when I see him and he acts hurtful toward me, I don't even care anymore. Maybe I am painting a picture of Quinn that is not real. But I know that You, oh Lord, can bless us and make our marriage what it should be. Lord, You are my only hope. I will do the only thing I know to do to prove to him that I am still serious about working on our marriage, regardless of the severe problems we are having.

Clarice grabbed her purse as she silently pleaded for help from her heavenly Father. She knew God cared. They had planned to talk about counseling for the kids today. But that could wait.

"Can we take a little walk?" she asked Quinn shyly.

"I don't feel like walking today."

Clarice was disappointed but she didn't know that Quinn had moved heavy furniture all day long and was exhausted.

"Well, we can meet another time," she said, her disappointment written all over her face.

"No that's okay," Quinn said. "I wanted to take you out to dinner at the Diner. Maybe we can take a walk after dinner when I've rested a little. I moved dozens of desks at work today and feel completely spent."

"Why didn't you say so in the first place? I thought you simply didn't care to spend time with me."

Quinn didn't comment. Clarice felt defeated. This man just didn't care or felt too superior to engage in "silly talk" like this. Why should she try?

There were so many things on her mind. She would have loved to share with him, but they probably wouldn't interest him anyway.

Lord, I feel angry right now. Why am I attracted to a man who doesn't really care about me or what I have to say? Please help me to look at You. I need to let him know that I still care. Besides, I yearn to be in his arms. The physical will have to do for now as it did for so long before I left him.

Quinn drove to the Diner and both were rather quiet while they ate.

"Let's go, I'll take you home," Quinn said, as he paid the bill.

Now or never, Clarice thought.

"Quinn, I actually wanted to talk to you. Can we go to your place for a while?"

"All right," Quinn said. They arrived at Quinn's apartment. "So what's up?" he asked Clarice.

"I...I...may I have some water please?"

Quinn brought her a glass of cold water and looked into her eyes. Clarice's face turned red.

"I wanted you to know that I still care for you and that you are the only man in my life. No one can deny that we have lots of problems, but I am willing and hoping to work on our marriage. I would like to do the counseling primarily for our marriage."

Quinn looked at Clarice and held her eyes.

"I...I wanted to show you that I still care very much. And if you also believe in working on our marriage then I...want to show you."

Quinn looked thoughtful. "I also would like to work on it. I," Quinn never finished the sentence. He just stared at Clarice who started to unbutton her shirt. Her hands shook a little and her face was still red. Quinn wanted to say something, anything. But no words would come out. He kept staring at Clarice as the last piece of clothing fell to the ground.

Clarice woke in Quinn's arms. He was looking right at her.

"How are you?" Quinn asked, as he gently pulled a strand of hair out of her face.

Clarice sighed, "I missed your closeness so much."

"Well that will change now. It's the end of the month, so I can give notice and move back by the end of next month."

Clarice looked panicked.

"What's wrong?" Quinn asked with a puzzled face.

"Quinn," Clarice said with tears in her eyes. "We are not ready for this yet."

"What do you mean, 'We're not ready?' Last night clearly showed that everything is fine."

"But it is not. We still need time to work on our marriage. There is so much that still has to change. And we have to find a way to come in agreement over the children."

Quinn sat up in bed and said in a cold voice, "I'll take you home now. Thank you for the pleasure last night," he added sarcastically.

Clarice sobbed, "Now I hurt you again and I only wanted to give us another chance."

"Hurting me is what you do best. Now get ready. I have other things to do."

Clarice didn't even bother to wash up. She slipped into her clothes, raked her hands through her hair and grabbed her purse. "Don't bother to take me home. I'll walk."

"No, I'll take you." But Clarice had already left the apartment before Quinn could get dressed and ready to go.

Oh Lord, what have I done? Clarice sobbed. *This whole situation is hopeless. And I wanted it to work out between us so badly. It simply can't end like this. I know where I can take my hurt. But Quinn is eaten up by it. The anger in him grows stronger with each misunderstanding. Lord, please heal his heart. Please forgive me for every hurt I caused him today and all the days that we've known each other. I want to see him free from all that anger. Lord he needs You. Please let him find You.*

Clarice could hardly see where she was going. Her vision was blurry from all the tears. It was very early in the morning and only a few cars were on the road. Thankfully Clarice's distress was unnoticed. She made her way home confused and disappointed.

Chapter Thirteen

A day had passed. Clarice felt sad and foolish. She was on the way to the grocery store but had to pull over. Tears blurred her vision. The pain was so deep within her heart that she could hardly stand it. Sobbing she screamed, *Lord, where are You? Why is this all happening? Don't You care? Why do You keep wisdom from me? Am I not Your child? Doesn't Your promise, "to receive wisdom freely if we only ask," apply to me? Am I a fool who has to walk in darkness? Lord, if You don't give me wisdom to deal with this impossible situation, I might as well die.*

Clarice dropped her head onto the steering wheel. Everything seemed so hopeless. She and Quinn had been separated for an entire year. Could God heal their marriage? Did He want to heal it? It didn't seem so. But Clarice knew deep down in her heart that God was well able to restore what seemed broken beyond repair. And then there were the visions. Would God fill her with hope just to take it away again? No. Clarice couldn't give up. She had to fight for her marriage. But how? *What do You want me to do? Please don't be silent dear God. Speak clearly to me.* Clarice felt drained. The tears stopped.

She looked to the mountains and remembered Psalm 121: *I lift my eyes to the hills – where does my help come from? My help comes from the Lord, maker of heaven and earth.*

With new resolve Clarice wiped her face dry. *I don't see the next step, but I know that You are with me. Your plans are good, oh Lord.*

Chapter Fourteen

Roger and Clarice had spent a lot of time together since Clarice's separation. Today he came to take a look at her newest paintings.

"Clarice, these are stunning." Roger said. "When did you paint these?"

"I started last week. This one is finished and the other one over here needs a little more work."

"You have to promise me that you will paint one for me, too."

Clarice smiled at Roger. "What if I tell you that it is done already?"

Roger stared at her with disbelief. "Why haven't you given it to me yet?"

"If I remember correctly, your birthday is coming up in a month."

"What? You will make me wait a whole month?"

"You bet," Clarice said with amusement. "Patience is a virtue."

"You have a way of torturing me," Roger said with a sigh. "What did Quinn say about your beautiful paintings?"

"I haven't shown him."

"Why not? I thought you were on speaking terms."

"That's true, but Quinn reproved me so harshly when I told him I planned to start painting that I don't want to share this special gift with him. He said I was arrogant to think I would become a famous painter. I never even claimed that I would be famous. I just followed God's calling. He doesn't understand that God talks to us in all kinds of ways."

"I'm sorry. But we both know that he is the one missing out."

"That's true. This walk with God is the most wonderful thing that ever happened to me. There is so much joy in knowing Christ. He has become my very best friend. And if I didn't trust Him so much, I would have never started to paint."

"You sure have a gift in painting."

"Believe me, this is a new thing. In school I was known as the stick figure artist. And my art pieces consisted of indistinguishable objects. That's why I was shocked when God called me to it."

"How exactly did God call you?"

"It started with a stranger who suggested I looked like a painter. I thought about my stick figure drawings and laughed inside. Then I kept hearing about that painting class on the radio. After being bombarded for a month from various sources I decided to check it out. It was a painting conference for five days out of town. I couldn't leave the kids that long and it also cost way too much. But when my pastor's dad came up to me after service and said out of the blue 'Aren't you the painter?' I knew that God spoke to me. I raised the money, asked a friend to watch the children, and went to the conference."

"This is so exciting, Clarice. God will bless you for your obedience in pursuing painting."

"Following God's calling is a blessing in itself. I feel like God moves my hands when I paint. It always reminds me that it is God's gift and not anything I do out of my own ability."

"Your paintings will touch many lives."

"That's the most exciting part of it all," Clarice said with shining eyes. "I want everything in my life to bring His love and His light to others."

"I can't wait to see all of this unfold," Roger said as he hugged Clarice.

"I just wish Quinn was a part of it. But as it is, I'm on my own."

"Clarice, if it doesn't work out with Quinn, you know how I feel about you."

"I know Roger. But I don't want you to be a replacement, just to fulfill my needs. You are way too special to me to do that to you. You deserve a wife who loves you for who you are and nothing less. You need to find a strong Christian woman to stay by your side, to work and support you as the pastor God calls you to be."

"Clarice, you are the strongest Christian woman I know."

Clarice sighed, "Let's just trust God in all of this."

The doorbell rang at the same time as the door opened and Isabelle and Lisa stormed into the living room. Fiona closed the door behind herself.

"Mom, Mom! The hippopotamus has a baby. We saw it swim in the water. It has eyes as big as this," Isabelle exclaimed as she widened her eyes.

"And the elephants sprayed us with water," Lisa said, "and we saw the lions being fed. One of them was roaring like this."

"That sounds wonderful," Clarice said, "but before you go on you should say hi to Uncle Roger."

"Hi Uncle Roger," Lisa said as Isabelle threw herself into his arms.

They really like him a lot, Clarice thought to herself as she watched them greet Roger. He squeezed both of them and made his way to the sofa. Isabelle jumped on his lap and Lisa cuddled on his side.

Clarice used this moment to make her way to Fiona's room. "Is everything all right?" she asked Fiona.

"Mom, they are so annoying. They wouldn't stop talking all the way home."

"I am sorry that you feel so bothered by that. In a way they remind me of a certain young lady in her earlier years," Clarice said with a twinkle in her eyes.

"Mom! Don't even say that I was like them."

"Okay, I won't say it. Thank you for taking them to the zoo. By the way, Uncle Roger is here and you should say hi to him."

"Do I have to? I'd rather listen to some music now."

"Just say hi. You can go right back to your room."

"Okay."

Isabelle and Lisa were still chatting about the zoo when Clarice and Fiona came to the living room. Fiona rolled her eyes at them. "Hi, Roger," she said as she turned around and left the room again.

"Hi, Fiona," Roger replied, knowing that she most likely didn't hear him. "*Teenagers,*" Clarice mouthed at him and received a grin from him in return. *I could see him in my life as more than just a good friend, she thought to herself. He understands my love for God, which is most important to me. Everything else would fall into place. Oh Lord, show me what to do!*

"I have to go now. I'm meeting with a friend for dinner," Roger said.

"Can we come?" Lisa and Isabelle beamed at him.

"No, unfortunately not. This will be a business meeting and female escorts are not allowed."

Lisa and Isabelle made long faces.

"How about a picnic after church this Sunday?"

"Oh yeah! Please, Mom. Can we?"

"I suppose so. Thanks for coming, Roger," Clarice agreed and hugged him goodbye.

"See you all Sunday," Roger said and left the house.

Chapter Fifteen

Clarice woke up in the middle of the night. *Lord, I am scared,* she prayed. *I don't know what to do. I don't make enough money to pay my bills. I haven't found a better job yet. Maybe I shouldn't have let my employer know that I am looking for a new job. But I felt I had to because my attitude toward work was becoming discontent and I hope it helped to let them know where I was coming from. Oh Lord, I am so very scared. I have to provide for my children but I need to be there for them as well. It seems there is no job out there for me which can give me the hours so I can be the provider but have the time to nurture them as well. I know there must be a perfect fit for me. But Lord, that's not all. I see a great disconnect to my older children. I simply am not interested in things of their world. I am drawn more to Christian songs and themes than to what they like. There is also hardly anything that Quinn and I have in common. Lord, help me to keep my eyes on You. For You and You alone are the answer to my despair. All these things I can't change out of my own strength. I know that You are the One who made heaven and earth and the universe. You created me and even though I am only a speck in Your creation, You care for me and have Your eye on me. Help me to trust in You. Help me to know You.*

Chapter Sixteen

Roger put the last dishes away. It had been a long day at work and a lonely dinner like so many before. *Oh Lord,* he prayed, *why am I still alone? I waited all these years to find the wife You have for me and feel like I am getting too old to get married. Is it Clarice You have for me? I know she wants her marriage still to work. But if her marriage ends in divorce, then I will pursue her. She is all I ever wished for.*

Roger went to the living room and turned on the news. But his thoughts kept wandering. He finally turned off the TV and opened his Bible. Just then the phone rang. Roger didn't feel like talking to anyone that late at night, but picked up the receiver anyways. "Hi," he said. There was no reply on the other end. Roger was about to hang up when he heard sobs. "Who is this?" he asked.

"It's me," Clarice managed to say.

"What has happened?" Roger asked. But instead of an answer there were more sobs.

"I'll be right over," Roger said and hung up the phone. His mind raced as he drove to Clarice's house. What could be wrong? Did anyone get hurt? He jumped out of his car and ran to the front door. Clarice opened her home to Roger. Her face was red from crying. He held her in a hug for a while and then guided her gently to the sofa.

"What's wrong?" he asked quietly after a while when the tears had stopped.

"Quinn has told me that he will divorce me next month. But that is not the worst. He told me that I will lose the house and will have to move into another place. That in itself wouldn't be a problem. I can make a home for myself wherever I go. But the children are safer here. This is a good neighborhood and we have great neighbors."

"Why does Quinn say you will lose the house?"

"He says we have too much debt, and I won't be able to hold the house."

Roger sat silently. He was angry with Quinn who yet again hurt his very best friend. He truly cared for Clarice and it was hard to see her in so much pain. What could he do? His thoughts came back to this evening when he considered a life with Clarice. If Quinn was going to divorce Clarice she would be free to marry again. Was this God's answer to his prayers? Was he to marry Clarice? Hope formed in his heart.

"Has Quinn given you the divorce papers yet?" Roger wanted to know.

"No," Clarice replied. "Somehow I hope he won't follow through with it. But I don't know what he will do. I have to be prepared for anything."

"I don't understand Quinn," Roger said. "Clarice I want you to know that you won't be alone in this. I will be at your side if Quinn follows through with the divorce."

"Thank you, Roger," Clarice said. She got up. "I better go to the bathroom and freshen up."

When she returned she sat down in the chair near the fireplace. "I am so glad you were able to come, Roger."

"I will always be there for you if you need me. Actually, I am jealous of Quinn. He doesn't know what a gift you are. I sure hope that Quinn sees that soon, or I might snatch you out of his hands."

"Roger, let's not start this again. I know exactly what attracts me to you. The joy and peace of the Lord is written all over your face. How can I not be drawn to a man like you? But I love Quinn. I believe with all my heart that God will turn his life around. I simply cannot give up on him."

"I know Clarice. I actually think that your devotion to your husband and to your marriage is the very thing I so admire about you."

"Thank you for your kind words. It is hard to wait. But this is all I can do. God has to reach Quinn. I can only wait."

"Here is a scripture for you Clarice. *Wait on the Lord and He will give you the desires of your heart.*'"

"Thanks Roger, I needed to hear that. Once when I was deceived many years ago, I learned that only God can open our eyes. He is the only one who can show Quinn the truth and can set him free. So I will have to wait."

Roger sighed. "Quinn is blessed beyond measure and doesn't even know it."

"Roger, I am not perfect. You make it seem like I could do nothing wrong."

"Well, Clarice, we all aren't perfect; but if a wife is devoted to the Lord the way you are, than even those imperfections will seem easy. I wish I had met you before Quinn did."

"You forget that I didn't know the Lord back then. Besides, I know that God has the perfect wife out there for you. It only takes patience. I have a hunch that she is already somewhere in your life. You deserve the very best."

"I sure hope she will be like you."

"Stop that talk, Roger. You have to be open for whomever God has for you. If you let Him guide you and if you wait on the Lord, I guarantee you, you won't be disappointed."

"I guess you're right." Roger sighed again.

"Of course I am," Clarice said with a twinkle in her eyes.

Roger smiled. "I am truly blessed to enjoy your friendship. I hope that our families will become close in the future."

"I sure hope so, too. You are my best friend and I know in my heart that you will be best friends with Quinn too, once he can call you his brother in the Lord. And God, in His loving way, will give you a wife who can become best friends with me."

"You know what? I really like that idea. Let's see God's plan unfold. I love you Clarice and I mean like a sister in Christ."

"That's better. I love you, too. I can't wait to meet your future wife."

"Tell me where she is and I will introduce you to her."

"That's God's job, not mine."

The doorbell rang. "I'll see who it is." Clarice opened the door and looked at the lady in the doorway. "Annette, is that you?" she exclaimed as she embraced her with a huge hug. Tears rolled down their cheeks. "I thought I would never see you again."

"Well you almost didn't. Oh Clarice, something wonderful has happened. I can't wait to tell you."

"You better come on in. I want you to meet a dear friend of mine."

"Oh you have company. I can come back another time."

"Nonsense! Come on in."

Annette followed Clarice into the living room. "Roger, I want you to meet my friend Annette. Annette, this is my very good friend Roger."

"It is nice to meet you, Annette! Have a seat."

"Nice to meet you too, Roger. I didn't want to intrude."

"You are not intruding," Clarice said sternly. "Now sit down. I'll go and fix us tea and sandwiches." Clarice disappeared into the kitchen.

"So where are you from?" Roger asked Annette after she sat comfortably.

"I am from here but moved many years ago to stay with my Mom. She lives in Colorado."

"So are you here for a visit or are you coming back to Albuquerque?"

"I am not sure yet. But I want to check out my job opportunities."

"Where are you working now?"

"I actually was working at the bank. But I quit my job last month to help my Mom."

Clarice entered the room with a serving tray holding steaming hot teacups and a plate filled with delicious sandwiches.

"You are simply the best," Roger said reaching for his favorite salmon sandwich.

"Annette and I used to spend a lot of time making all kinds of different sandwiches. Once we entertained our whole high school senior class, teachers included."

"I remember that because we experimented with cream cheese-green chili paste for the party," Annette said. "The green chili was supposed to be medium-hot but that year a medium chili was more like a super hot one!"

"Yes," Clarice started laughing. "And our beloved biology teacher came and tried it. She didn't see the chili and after her first bite her eyes watered. I could see flames coming from her mouth and ears."

"And then she drank water which made it only worse," Annette burst out. "We finally saved her and gave her milk to soothe her mouth and throat."

"Teachers don't get paid enough for what they go through in and out of their classrooms," Roger said laughing.

"I am glad that she took the incident with humor," Clarice said. "We are still in contact. By the way, she asked about you, Annette."

"Tell her hi from me when you see her," Annette said.

They all shared funny memories of their high school years and didn't realize the time.

"Oh no," Roger shrieked. "It's one o'clock and I have to be at work early tomorrow, I mean today. I better get going. It was nice to meet you, Annette," Roger said shaking Annette's hand.

"Same here," Annette replied.

Clarice walked Roger to the door. "Take care," she said and hugged him.

"Bye," Roger said and made his way to the car.

Clarice closed the door and went back to the living room.

"I should get going, too," Annette said.

"Where are you staying?" Clarice asked.

"Probably at a motel for tonight," Annette said putting on her jacket.

"No," Clarice said. "It's too late to find a place. You can have the sofa."

"Are you sure that Quinn will be okay with it?" Annette asked.

"Quinn doesn't live here anymore. I separated from him."

"Oh, I am sorry. What happened?"

"Well it's a long story. We better talk about it later."

"Thank you for letting me stay. I came straight from the airport to you, but didn't plan to stay so long."

"I am glad you came. I often wondered what became of you. Let me get you a blanket and pajamas. It looks like we are still the same size."

"Thank you," Annette said and took the dishes into the kitchen. She rinsed them off and loaded them into the dishwasher. *This is just like old days*, she thought. *If only I had not made all those wrong choices, we could have enjoyed our friendship all of these past years. Well, at least we are friends again.*

"Here we go," Clarice said to Annette and handed her a towel. "Your pajamas are on the sofa. Please help yourself if you need anything."

"Thanks Clarice. I am so happy to be here."

"I always hoped to see you again," Clarice said hugging Annette. "We have to talk tomorrow when the kids are at school."

Annette changed into her pajamas and lay down on the soft sofa. She fell asleep when her head touched the pillow.

Chapter Seventeen

"Mom, where are my shoes?" Norbert yelled from his room.
"Wherever you left them yesterday," Clarice replied.

"Very funny," Norbert yelled again. "I can't find them. Can you please help me?"

"In a minute," Clarice said. She didn't want to get up. The late night allowed her only four hours of sleep. She rolled over in her bed and was about to doze off again. *Oh no*, Clarice thought. *He is going to wake Annette.* Clarice jumped out of her bed and went quickly to Norbert's room. "Please be as quiet as possible this morning. We have a visitor sleeping on the sofa."

"Who?" Norbert asked curiously.

"Annette, a friend from high school."

Just then Clarice's alarm went off. She hurried to her bedside and quieted it. I may as well get up now, she decided. After a long warm shower she felt better. She chose her favorite every-day dress and went to the kitchen.

"You found your shoes," she said to Norbert who sat in front of a bowl of cereal. "Where were they?"

"Under my bed. Where is Fiona? She is usually up before me."

"I'll check," Clarice said and went to Fiona's room. "What's up sleepyhead? Aren't you going to get up today?"

"What time is it?" Fiona asked sleepily.

"6:45 a.m."

"Oh no!" Fiona screamed and jumped out of bed. She rushed to the bathroom.

Clarice went back to the kitchen knowing that Fiona would be ready in

Superman speed. She made herself some tea and prepared the evening's food for the slow cooker. That way she could spend more time with Annette.

Fiona rushed through the kitchen grabbing a granola bar and was out the door barely yelling "bye" over her shoulder.

Norbert was annoyed. "How come she wakes up later than me and is gone before me?" He grabbed his book bag and made his way to the door. "Bye, Mom," he managed to mumble.

"Bye, Norbert," Clarice said.

Silence filled the house again. Clarice took her tea and sat down at the table with her Bible. Mornings were her favorite time to spend with the Lord. It was more refreshing than the shower she had taken.

Seven thirty came around and the little ones had to get up. Clarice put her Bible away and went to the kid's room. Lisa was already reading. After many years of struggles, she had learned to read and was now inseparable from books.

Isabelle was still fast asleep. She was her night owl who would stay up all night and sleep all day if she could.

"Rise and shine," Clarice said gleefully.

Lisa looked at her: "Can I finish this page before getting up?"

"No," Clarice said. "You have to get ready for school first. If you still have enough time left, you may read some more."

"But Isabelle is still sleeping."

"Not much longer," Clarice said as she tickled Isabelle's tummy.

"Leave me alone. I'm tired," Isabelle responded.

Clarice continued tickling Isabelle mercilessly while Isabelle squirmed around. Finally she withdrew from Isabelle saying, "You better get up within the next five minutes or the tickle monster will return."

Clarice went back to the kitchen and set bowls, cereal and milk on the table. "Oh, you are awake," she said when Annette entered the kitchen. "I'm surprised you were able to sleep through all that noise early this morning."

"I was quite tired," Annette said. "Do you still make that delicious tea?"

"Of course. I think I should let you in on the secret ingredients in the tea. I add a fresh lemon mint leaf and one teaspoon of cinnamon honey to every cup of tea. As a matter of fact I can make you a cup right now."

"I would like that a lot. I missed our tea parties," Annette said. "So many years passed by and I don't know why I waited this long to finally come to you and ask your forgiveness."

"Sometimes it is hard to do so. You never know how the other one will react. But I am very glad you came. I prayed for our friendship to be restored."

Clarice brewed a pot of tea and set two cups on the table. "Let's sit down and enjoy the tea together like the old days."

Just then Lisa came to the table her nose in her book. She didn't see the guest and sat down.

"Lisa, this is Miss Annette," Clarice said. "Annette this is my little bookworm Lisa."

Lisa looked curiously at Annette. "How come she is wearing your pajamas?" she wanted to know.

"Did I hear a 'Good morning Miss Annette'?" Clarice addressed Lisa.

"Oops," Lisa said. "Hi, Miss Annette."

"Nice to meet you, Lisa," Annette replied. "Your Mom told me that you love books."

"I do. They are so much fun."

"What book are you reading now?" Annette asked.

"Wake That Sleepy Monster."

Clarice jumped up. "I bet Isabelle is still sleeping and she has to be at school in fifteen minutes."

Lisa helped herself to some cereal while Clarice rushed to the kid's bedroom. "Isabelle, are you awake?" But instead of an answer Clarice heard a soft snoring noise. *This little stinker*, Clarice thought and tickled her. "You really have to get up, or we will be late for school," Clarice said while she pulled the blanket off.

Isabelle gave up the fight and went to the bathroom to brush her teeth.

"You have to be very fast because school starts in ten minutes."

"Why did you wake me so late?" Isabelle complained.

Clarice just sighed and went back to the kitchen. "I have to take the girls to school," she told Annette. "You can take a shower in the back bathroom."

"Thanks, Clarice," Annette said.

Isabelle came into the kitchen, looking curiously at Annette. "This is Miss Annette, my friend."

"Hi, I am Isabelle. Are you coming to school with us?"

"No. But I will see you after school."

"Talking about school," Clarice interrupted, "We have to go now or we will be late."

"But I didn't have breakfast yet," Isabelle protested.

"Just take a granola bar. We really have to go." Clarice took her purse and went out the door. Both girls grabbed their backpacks and ran after her.

After Clarice dropped off the girls she took a deep breath. *Another hectic morning*, she thought. But she was very eager to go back home to spend some time with Annette and catch up on all those years they hadn't seen each other.

Annette had taken her shower and was ready for the day when Clarice entered the house. "Let me make us a fresh cup of tea. The other one is already cold," Clarice said while she filled the kettle with water. When the tea was ready, they sat in the garden with their cups in their hands. "Are all your mornings that busy?" Annette wanted to know.

"Typically yes," Clarice responded. "But today was one of the busiest. The kids sure keep me hopping."

"You seem very happy," Annette said.

"I am very happy. The children bring me much joy; even so, there are some difficult days in between."

"And what about Quinn? You said you are separated."

"Yes. I told him to move out. Sometimes I ask myself why I did it. I still love him. But I simply can't live like this anymore. Quinn can be the greatest guy in the world but the next moment he acts angry and distant. I couldn't take the behavior. We always had difficulties about how to discipline the children. I can't take his put downs and the put downs of the children anymore. Family life is supposed to be happy. But we always had a dark cloud over us. I never knew if Quinn was going to be friendly or angry. He never hit me but the way he disciplined the children made me very uncomfortable. I know that I am not perfect. I would need Quinn's help with disciplining the children; but his way of disciplining them was unacceptable to me."

"I am very sorry," Annette said. "I wish I could help you."

"I tried so hard for many years when we were still together. But I finally came to the conclusion that I can't turn things around. That's why I had to separate. Only God has the power to change our situation and to reconcile us. That is my deepest wish. Sometimes I wonder though if God has different plans for my life."

"Time will tell," Annette said.

"But enough about me. You said yesterday that something wonderful has happened."

"Yes indeed. Over the years I heard that you started a 'weird new thing'. People from our high school years told me that you became a fanatic Christian. I was glad that we weren't in contact anymore. A weirdo didn't fit into my life. Then I went to live with my mom. On the way there I had a lady sitting next to me in the airplane who asked me what church I go to. When I told her that I don't attend church, she started to tell me her life story. If anyone ever had a hard life, it was her. She said that Jesus helped her all of the way and that He stood by her side in every situation she had to face. I was relieved when we finally arrived at our destination. All that 'God talk' made me uncomfortable.

"Last year mom came down with cancer and they gave her treatments. I was in total shock. Just the word 'cancer' has given me chills all my life. And now my mom had it. I was desperate. One Sunday morning I went for a walk. I just couldn't stay inside and encourage my mom while I was hurting so much. And walking had always helped me in the past. But that day I just couldn't feel better. I ended up in front of a church and felt something drawing me inside. A church was the last place I wanted to be. If there was a God, He definitely didn't care about me. But there I was. I sat down in the back. The pastor talked about Jesus our Healer. He said that Jesus cares about us even when bad things happen in our life. He said that He has not forgotten about us and that He is with us in every situation. He wants to comfort us. Then the pastor gave the altar call. I stood up and went forward. I was so desperate for comfort that I decided to give this thing a try. When the pastor prayed over me, I felt a warmth and comfort inside that I can't describe. I knew that something had happened that was beyond my own self. A lady came up to me after the service and invited me to a Bible Study at her house. She also gave me a Bible. From that day on I was a changed person."

"I am so happy for you," Clarice said. "I have prayed for you ever since I was saved."

"I sincerely thank you for all your prayers. I don't know what I would do without the Lord."

"Did your mom get better?"

"At first yes. She had to go through chemotherapy. That was one of the toughest things for me to watch. She felt very sick from the drugs and, at the end, she lost her hair. But the cancer was in remission and she felt better every day. Then just a month ago, the cancer came back. The doctors say she has only a year to live."

"I am very sorry, Annette."

Annette dried off a tear with her sleeve. "I felt overwhelmed with everything. I needed to get away from it all for a while. But I didn't allow myself to do so. Mom must have sensed it. She encouraged me to go on a little vacation. We talked about it and Mom suggested looking you up. She always liked you a lot."

"I am glad she thought of me. As I said, I missed you very much. Maybe I can come with you to visit your mom when you go back home."

"Mom would be delighted to see you."

Clarice sighed. "I wish there was something I could do for you."

"There is nothing anyone can do." Tears rolled down Annette's cheeks.

Clarice embraced her friend and prayed silently for God's strength to fill Annette.

When Annette felt better, they went for a long walk. They enjoyed walking a lot. It filled them with peace and lifted their spirits. They made it back just in time to pick up Isabelle and Lisa.

"Can I come along?" Annette asked.

"Of course. The girls will be happy to see you."

Both girls were already waiting in front of the school building. Isabelle smiled when she saw that their guest came along to pick them up. Lisa had a sour face.

"Hi, girls. How was school?" Clarice asked hoping that Lisa would tell her what made her so unhappy. Instead Lisa sat down and looked out the window. Isabelle on the other hand, had thousands of stories to tell. Her most favorite thing at this point was to chase after boys and being chased by them. "Tyler ran after me in all of our breaks," she said excitedly. "He is so annoying but at the same time so cute."

"Do I hear wedding bells?" Clarice teased.

"Mom, that's not funny," Isabelle yelled. "Besides I am going to marry Johnny."

"Ah!" Clarice exclaimed.

Roger's car was in front of the house when they arrived. "Uncle Roger," Isabelle yelled and ran into his arms.

"Hi, young lady," he picked her up and twirled her around. "Hi Clarice, hi Annette," he said when he placed Isabelle back on the ground. "What's wrong with Lisa?" he asked.

"I don't know yet. I bet she went straight to her room. Please excuse me."

Clarice walked up the driveway to the house and made her way to Lisa's room. Lisa lay on her bed crying.

"What's wrong?" Clarice asked and pulled her into her arms.

"I studied so hard for the spelling test and ended up with a 'C.'"

Clarice stroke her hair. "That's okay. Did you know that spelling was one of my weakest subjects in school?"

"Really? But you always know how to spell words when I ask you."

"My spelling improved over the years."

"But I won't ever learn it."

"Who knows? Besides, some of the greatest geniuses don't know how to spell."

"Really?"

"Really!" Clarice embraced Lisa. "Did you see that Uncle Roger is here? Why don't you wash your face and say hi to him."

"Thanks, Mom," Lisa said and hurried to the bathroom.

Roger, Isabelle and Annette sat in the living room. Clarice entered the room. "Isabelle, please set the table," she said. "We'll have an early dinner. Roger, I hope you can stay."

"Yes, I can. I was going to invite you all for some ice cream after dinner."

"Hi, Uncle Roger," Lisa said. "Did I hear ice cream?"

"Hi, young lady. And yes you heard right. I will take you all out for some ice cream after dinner."

"Yay!" Lisa yelled.

"I have to check on Norbert and Fiona. They should be home already." Clarice looked in their rooms. They weren't there. She went to the kitchen and saw a note. "I'll have to go to the gym and pick up Norbert and Fiona. They left me a note that they were checking out the membership prices. They have been fighting like crazy lately and I am glad they found something nice to do together."

"No problem, Clarice," Roger said. "We'll hold down the fort until you are back."

"Can I come with you?" Annette asked.

"Okay. Let's go." Together they drove off. "I was thinking, Annette. Why don't you stay with us while you are in town?"

"I would love to, but Mom arranged for me to stay with an old friend of hers. I am supposed to be there by eight tonight."

"Okay. But you have to promise me that you visit us often."

"I promise. I am so glad that we are finally connected again."

"Me, too. I missed you so much."

"Roger seems to be a fine fellow."

"He is. I know him from church. He has become a very dear friend to me. And he has supported me a lot since my separation from Quinn."

"You would make a nice couple."

"At times I think that too. But I love Quinn and want to see my marriage restored more than anything."

"I'll pray for you."

"Thank you," Clarice said and parked the car in front of the fitness center. Fiona and Norbert were already waiting.

"What took you so long?" Norbert asked annoyed.

"We had to wait forever," Fiona said with attitude.

"You better watch yourselves. Besides I didn't even know that you were here until I found the note." *Teenagers*, Clarice thought. But she wasn't going to let these two moody teens take the joy away that Clarice felt in seeing her friend. She chose to concentrate on Annette instead who was silently praying for this situation.

After dinner Roger took them to the ice cream parlor. They returned to the house for a cup of coffee. Fiona and Norbert went to their rooms while

Lisa and Isabelle had some hot chocolate. The evening was spent with lots of laughter and stories from the past.

"We have to do this again," Roger said to Annette. "You are revealing a whole lot about Clarice I didn't know."

"Sounds like a plan," Annette winked at Roger.

"Don't you dare tell him all the embarrassing stuff about me. There are some nice stories I can tell him about you, too. Like the one with the cake," Clarice threatened with a twinkle in her eye.

"Not the one with the cake," Annette pleaded, bending over with laughter.

"I hate to say it, but I need to go," Roger said as he got up to fetch his jacket. "See you all later."

Lisa and Isabelle, who had taken in all the fun listening, ran to Roger and gave him a big hug.

After Roger had left, Annette looked at her watch and exclaimed, "It's already eight ten. Could you please give me a ride. It's really close to here."

"Of course I can," Clarice said. "Lisa and Isabelle, I want to see you in bed when I return."

"Okay, Mom," they said reluctantly.

Clarice and Annette arrived at a pretty little house with roses in front of it. The friend of Annette's mom was very kind and showed Annette to her room.

When Annette settled in for the night, she found herself thinking about Roger. He was different from all the other guys she had met. The image of his smiling face popped up in her mind and her stomach did a belly flop. *That's ridiculous*, she reprimanded herself. *I am acting like a little schoolgirl in love. After all, I just met the guy.* But the more she fought her feelings the stronger they got. Annette fell asleep with Roger on her mind.

Chapter Eighteen

Annette's cheeks felt hot again. Why couldn't she control herself? Roger kept his gaze on her, which didn't help.

"Let's have dessert," Clarice said. "Lisa and Isabelle please help me clear the table. Fiona, please get the plates and forks. I'll fetch the pie and ice cream."

"Take the cups to the kitchen. I'll take the plates," Lisa told Isabelle.

"You're not my boss," Isabelle protested.

"Stop arguing and just get the job done," Clarice intervened.

"I'll get the coffee," Annette said, trying to escape Rogers gaze.

Roger leaned back in his chair with a slight smile on his face. He really liked Annette. Her hair had a golden shine to it, which complemented her hazel eyes. She was intelligent, loving and caring. And most of all, her belief in God was authentic. When she talked about the Lord, Roger could feel the intimate relationship she shared with Jesus. Could Annette be the one for him? He had only known her for two weeks. Something deep within stirred and warmed him from the inside out.

I designed Annette to be your wife. Together you will serve Me.

Roger was startled. "*Lord, was that You?*" There was no answer, but a deep assurance in his heart that Annette was the one for him. Never in a million years would he have expected to know beyond the shadow of a doubt who his wife was going to be. Roger had heard of a few men who laid eyes on a woman and knew that God had chosen that woman for them. He was still deep in thought when the table was ready and Clarice served the apple pie while Norbert added a big scoop of vanilla ice cream to each plate. Annette poured coffee for Clarice, Roger and herself. Her hands were a little shaky. *Get a grip*, she told herself but it didn't make any difference. Annette ate a piece of pie even though she didn't feel like eating. Her stomach felt like it was full of butterflies. Roger couldn't keep his eyes off of her.

"Why does Uncle Roger keep staring at Annette?" Isabelle asked curiously.

"How does the pie taste?" Clarice tried to divert the question.

Roger turned to Clarice, "It is very tasty. Who made it?"

"My friend Lydia baked it for us. She is quite the dessert queen. If you ever need a pie or cheese cake, you know whom to ask," Clarice said.

"Uncle Roger," Lisa said. "You should have been here last week. Miss Lydia brought over the best cheese cake ever."

"I was only allowed to eat one piece," Isabelle said.

"Well that was plenty for your little body," Clarice laughed. "If it was up to you, you would have eaten the whole cake."

"Besides, we wanted some too," Fiona said, making a face at her sister.

Annette was very quiet during the meal and stole little glimpses of Roger here and there. Once their eyes met and locked for a few seconds. Annette could feel her cheeks burn and her stomach making summer saults. She was excited and embarrassed at the same time. Annette felt drawn to this man. He was good-looking, tall with dark brown hair and a charming smile. But that wasn't primarily what attracted her to him. There was something in his gaze. He had peace, joy and compassion in his eyes. Annette tried to put her thoughts aside. Even though she liked Roger a lot, she knew that he deserved better. There was no chance for the two of them, not after what she had done. Hurtful memories tried to invade her thoughts. If only she could change the past. If only she could have made better choices. But it was too late now. Still she couldn't help the deep feelings toward Roger that made her want to laugh and cry at the same time.

"Let's sit in the living room," Clarice's voice interrupted Annette's thoughts.

Isabelle tugged on Roger's arm. "Can you read me a story?" she asked him with cute puppy eyes that no one could refuse.

"Of course," he grinned back at her, knowing that she had him wrapped around her little finger and that there was no room for a "no."

Annette and Clarice sat next to each other on the sofa while Isabelle hopped on Roger's lap on the rocking chair. She had brought a whole stack of books to read and chose her favorite about a bear named Puck. Lisa lay on the floor and listened to the story while drawing in her notebook. Norbert and Fiona went to their rooms.

"So how is your Mom doing?" Clarice asked Annette.

"Not so good," Annette answered. "I called her yesterday. She should have knee surgery, but her overall health is so bad that the doctors don't want to risk it."

"Has the cancer spread?"

"Yes. They found traces of it in her liver."

"I am so sorry," Clarice said as she laid her hand on Annette's. "Is there anything I can do?"

"Pray. That's the only hope we have." Annette answered. "What is hardest for me is that Mom doesn't know the Lord yet."

"Oh, Annette. That must be difficult for you."

"It is indeed. She rejects everything I tell her about the Lord. I don't know how to witness to her."

"The changes in you and in your life are a great witness for the Lord. Surely she must see that."

"I don't know Clarice. It seems like she has no open mind for anything other than her anger and disappointment about her life and her sickness."

"I will pray that God will show His goodness to her and that He will surround her with his love."

"Thanks Clarice. I am thankful to have you as my friend."

"I am thankful for you too," Clarice said and hugged Annette.

Isabelle and Lisa had left after the bear story to play in their room. Roger heard what Annette had said about her mom's cancer and that her Mom wasn't saved yet. It moved him deeply. He himself was blessed with strong Christian parents who devoted their lives to the Lord as young teenagers. Both had served as missionaries in Africa and that's where they met. Roger spent his early childhood in South Africa and witnessed many miracles. When he was five years of age his parents moved to Albuquerque, New Mexico where he went to school and graduated from high school. He then went to the University of Colorado. Every other weekend he drove home to spend time with his parents. In his fourth year of college his dad was diagnosed with cancer. Roger interrupted his studies to support his mom and spent time with his dad. The cancer was in its last stages when it was found, which left only a couple of months for his dad to live. It was a painful but also a joyful time they experienced, for they all knew that once Dad died, he would be welcomed into the everlasting presence of Jesus.

Annette didn't have that comfort. Roger committed in his heart to pray for Annette's mother's salvation every day.

"I am so very sorry, Annette," Roger said with compassion in his eyes. "This must be very hard for you."

"It is," Annette answered realizing that Roger must have heard most of their conversation.

A silence fell between them. Roger's voice broke the silence as he prayed, "Dear Heavenly Father. We bring before you Annette's mom and ask You to comfort her and to let her get to know You. May she accept Your free gift of salvation. In Jesus' name we pray. Amen."

When Roger turned to Annette, her eyes were filled with tears. "Thank you, Roger. You don't know how much your prayer means to me," Annette said softly. Silence filled the room again.

"I need to go," Annette said after a few minutes.

"Did you drive here?" Clarice asked.

"No. I walked," Annette answered.

"Can I give you a ride home?" Roger offered.

"No, I'd rather walk. The air is nice and fresh and not too warm at this time of year, and I enjoy walking on such nights."

"In that case, may I walk you home?" Roger asked.

Annette blushed. "I would like that," she said, her heart racing.

"I will get your jackets and let the kids know that you are leaving," Clarice said as she left the living room. Norbert was already asleep.

"You can't leave already!" Isabelle protested as she ran into Roger's arms.

"I have to. But I will come by again soon," Roger said as he hugged Isabelle.

"Don't forget the soccer game on Saturday," Lisa yelled. "Daddy said we are playing against the 'White Tigers'."

"I'll be there," Roger assured the girls. "Bye, Fiona. You are quite a helper for your mom."

"We are too," the little ones said in unison.

"Of course you are," Roger laughed at the demand of acknowledgement.

"Bye," the kids said to Annette and hugged her. Annette had watched with admiration how affectionately Roger dealt with the girls and how they in return showed him their love.

Clarice handed the jackets to Annette and Roger.

"May I help you?" Roger asked as he took Annette's jacket from her and held it so she could slide in.

"Thank you," Annette said, blushing again.

"Bye you guys. See you later," Clarice said and hugged them both.

Fiona smiled at her Mom after the door closed behind Roger and Annette. "Do I hear wedding bells?" she asked with a twinkle in her eyes.

"You never know," Clarice said amused. "But I have a feeling you might be right."

Lisa and Isabelle had run into their room again. And that was a good thing...

Chapter Nineteen

Roger and Annette walked side by side down the street. The night air was very pleasant and stars started to sparkle in the dark night sky.

"I love to walk in the peace and quiet of the night," Annette sighed.

"I enjoy walking, too," Roger said. "When I was a young boy my parents took me on night walks in the woods."

"Weren't you scared?" Annette asked.

"No. I knew that my dad was going to protect Mom and me."

"It must be nice to have your dad watch out for you."

"Didn't your dad watch out for you?" Roger asked.

"My father wasn't around much, and when he was home, he would be drunk and beat my mom."

Roger stopped walking. He turned his face to Annette. "I am truly sorry, Annette. No one should ever have to live like that."

"I used to cry a lot. But it is okay now. After I found the Lord I realized that He always watches over us and is always with us. Unfortunately, Mom never understood. When I tell her that Jesus is ever present she asks where He was when she was beaten."

"Have you read the story about the footprints?" Roger asked.

"Yes. I had just accepted Christ when a friend told it to me. It is one of my most favorite stories."

They came to the park and sat down on a bench.

"Life is not always easy," Annette said, "but with the Lord, it is meaningful. I don't know how I ever lived without him."

"My parents walked close with the Lord. My greatest desire was to do the same, and by His grace He granted it to me. I feel His presence like a warm blanket over my life. It is difficult for me to see people without that comfort and peace."

"I sometimes want to stop everyone on the street, to let them know how much Jesus loves them and that He wants to be their Lord and Savior."

"That's the Father's heart. He must be pleased when He looks down on you. He gave you the gift of compassion."

Annette looked up into the sky. "I never understood people who said that they loved God. It sounded so weird. But when Jesus got ahold of my life, everything changed. I love Him more than anything." Annette sighed. "I think I have to get home now. It is already very late."

They walked in the quiet of the night until they finally stood in front of Annette's place. "Thank you for walking me home."

"It was my pleasure," Roger said and waited until she closed the door behind her. *Oh Lord, she is beautiful. Show me how to pursue her. I don't want to scare her off.* He walked back to his car and drove home.

Chapter Twenty

Clarice opened the door. "Come on in," she said to Maeve, a co-worker at her new job. "Lunch is ready."

"Thank you so much for inviting me. I like your house," she said as she sat down.

"I can give you a tour later."

They ate their chef salads which Clarice had prepared for them. When they were finished, Clarice showed Maeve around.

Maeve looked excitedly at Clarice's windows. "They sparkle, just like you always sparkle."

Clarice chuckled. "I understand what you mean when you say that my windows sparkle. But I don't sparkle; I haven't even taken a shower yet."

"It's not the outside. It's something more. Even though I've only known you a short time it is evident to me that the separation from Quinn is hard on you. And still I sense a joy and peace in you. It shows in your eyes and in your smiles."

"Well it is similar to the sparkle in my windows. I washed my windows with a solution of hot water and vinegar, and rinsed them with clear hot water. That way my windows are clean from all the dirt."

"I'll try that. I want my windows to sparkle too. But how do you manage to sparkle from the inside?"

"It is because I have been cleansed too, by blood."

"You creep me out. What do you mean by blood?"

"You see, we all are sinners, we are born with sin. And the only way to get cleansed from that sin is by the blood of Jesus."

"But He died a long time ago."

"Yes He did. He died on the cross to pay for all of our sins. Our sins are washed away by His blood."

"How can a dead person do anything for you?"

"Jesus is not dead. God raised Him from the dead. He is alive and sits in heaven at the right hand of the Father."

"But then He is still gone."

"Through the Holy Spirit He lives in us, if we open our hearts to Him."

"That's confusing. I just don't get it. Who is the Holy Spirit? I thought you spoke about Jesus. And what's that thing about the Father? Joseph was Jesus' father and died too."

"Those are good questions. Let me try to explain. Your mom, your dad, your brother and you are a family. You are all the Tylers. Now the Father, the Son and the Holy Spirit are kind of like a family too. They are God."

"Who is the most important? The Father?"

"Actually they are equally important. They all are God."

"I just don't get it."

"It's like with water. Water is H_2O. It can be steam, liquid, or ice. But it is always H_2O. The Father, Jesus and the Holy Spirit are all God."

"But Jesus was a man and walked on this earth."

"That's true, Jesus was fully man. But He was also fully God."

"But if He was fully God, He could have gotten off that cross and saved His life. I mean, how could nails hold down God?"

"Nails didn't. It was His great love for us that kept Him on the cross. Jesus knew that only through His death on the cross we humans could be reconciled to God. Even in the garden of Gethsemane He prayed, If there is any other way then let this pass by. But there wasn't. That's why He died for us, for you and me."

"But you don't need the blood of Jesus. You are a good person. You would make it into heaven for sure."

"God is a righteous God. His standards are so high that even a bad thought separates us from Him. We all are guilty and deserve death. Jesus died in our place so that we can spend eternity with Him. Through His cleansing blood, shed on the cross, we became clean and acceptable before God and can spend eternity with Him."

"To be honest, I don't quite understand all this."

"I know it is kind of confusing. Why don't you take this Bible and read it. It has some helpful remarks added. They helped me when I started reading the Bible. You are also welcome to come to church with us. And don't feel shy to ask me any questions. If I can't answer them, we can ask the pastor."

"Thank you. I will think about it. Thanks for lunch."

"You are welcome and see you at work tomorrow."

"Bye, Clarice."

Thank you for the opportunity to share Your truth with Maeve, Clarice prayed as she closed the door behind her. *Help Maeve to know You and accept You as Lord and Savior.*

Chapter Twenty-one

"I feel really double minded," Clarice said to Lydia. "On the one hand I would like to reconcile with Quinn. After all, I still love him and we have four children together. He will always be the father of my children, and it would be so much easier for them, if we were together. But on the other hand…" Clarice stared into space, almost forgetting that Lydia was there. Lydia sat patiently as always, giving Clarice the time she needed to deal with her thoughts.

"I think he didn't really love her," Clarice suddenly said.

Lydia stared at Clarice: "What do you mean?"

"About a year after we were separated Quinn had a girlfriend. He brought her to a family picnic and introduced her as a co-worker."

"That must have been very difficult. Did you know right away…that she was his girlfriend?"

"I suspected it. It's just that I didn't think Quinn would be that inconsiderate to bring her to a family event. I didn't tell anyone because it disturbed me too much. I also had to work through my fears about the children possibly dealing with a step-mom. I understand that Quinn didn't want to be alone anymore, and being separated from me for so long…he just went on with his life. But," a tear formed at Clarice's eye, "I am sure he did sleep with her, and I don't know how many other women. Even so, we are still married. 'It's over with her,' he said, but every time he says he's going to the apartment to sleep, I suspect that he's meeting up with another woman. It's incredible how much an affair can damage the trust between two people." Clarice took a sip of her tea. "I shouldn't even dwell on any of this. He said he will divorce me anyway, and that his relationship with the other woman is over."

Lydia touched Clarice's hand. "Don't give up yet. God is a big God, and if it is in His will, He will turn things around."

"I know, Lydia. But I don't want to hold on to false hope. Besides, this marriage is such a mess; I don't want to go back to what it was. I want my marriage and my family healed, not just reunited. There are so many issues I don't want to live with anymore. I have a legitimate need to be respected, and being disrespected and demeaned gets me very angry. Do you know how it feels to be called a child by your own husband just because you disagree with his decisions or his approach to disciplining the kids?"

"No, I don't know how it feels, and he should never do that to you. You have proven so often that you are a capable woman, mother and wife and I only can imagine how it hurts to be put down by the one who should stand by you as an equal partner."

"Equal-- that's how it should be," Clarice said with tears streaming down her cheeks. "Why does he have to put me down? It makes me feel insecure. I know that he sometimes uses it to manipulate me. When I finally realized that he manipulates my decisions by making me feel bad, a part of my love and respect for him died."

Clarice stared into space again. After a long moment Lydia touched Clarice's hand. "Don't give up, Clarice. I truly feel that the victory is around the corner. It's not an accident that you found Quinn's wedding ring after he had thrown it away. I believe God used this as a sign among many others you shared with me."

"I know and I am holding on to them. I need to trust God's power to heal my family and my marriage. But as I said, I feel double minded at times."

"Just remember that all things are possible with God. Ask God to help you forgive Quinn and also yourself. There is power in forgiveness."

"It is interesting that you talk about forgiveness. I hear a song about forgiveness almost every time I turn on the radio. And now you confirm it." Clarice looked straight at Lydia, "Will you please pray for me in your quiet time for God to help me forgive? I am tired of holding on to unforgiveness."

"I sure will," Lydia said and squeezed Clarice's hand.

"I feel blessed to know you, Lydia. God's favor is on me by surrounding me with friends like you."

"I am blessed to know you too, Clarice. I thank God for our friendship daily." Lydia checked her watch. "I need to go now. See you at church and keep your head up. God is in control."

"Thanks, Lydia. I will."

Chapter Twenty-two

Annette sat at the kitchen table. "I need to go back to Mom's. She is feeling worse and I have rested up enough to face the challenge of taking care of her again."

"We will miss you. Have you told Roger?"

"No, and I plan to leave without telling him."

"Why? He seems to be very fond of you."

"I like him a lot, too. But it can't be."

"What do you mean 'it can't be'? Neither of you has any commitment to anyone else and I personally would like to see you both together."

"It would be nice. But I did too many bad things in the past. It is just not possible."

"Believe me, Annette, the past is the past and you don't have to be hindered by it."

"Please stop, Clarice. It simply can't be. I will leave this afternoon. I just wanted to say goodbye. Tell the kids that I will miss them."

"Do you need a ride to the train station?"

"That would be nice. And please don't tell Roger."

"When does your train leave?"

"In an hour. I have already packed."

"Maybe I should take you right now so you don't miss the train."

"That would probably be best."

Clarice and Annette drove to the station, and Clarice parked the car.

"You don't have to wait around," Annette said.

"Are you kidding. I want to spend these last moments with you. After all, we didn't see each other for years and a couple of weeks are hardly enough to make up for that time. When will you come again?"

"I don't know yet. It depends on how Mom does. Here is her address and phone number if you need to get in contact with me."

"Thanks and say hi to your mom from me."

"I will and thanks for everything. I am so happy to have you back in my life again."

"I am happy to have you back in my life again, too. Take care and call me soon."

Annette got on the train. Clarice watched her sadly. *I miss her already*, she thought.

When Clarice arrived back home Roger's car was in front of the house. "Hey there," he said as he got out of the car. "Is Annette coming over today? I was planning to show her the zoo this Saturday."

"Unfortunately, she is gone. Her mom's condition got worse."

"Why didn't she say goodbye?" he asked pacing the driveway.

"She was in a rush and had to go immediately."

"When is she coming back?"

"I don't know. I guess she will stay with her mom till the end of this cancer battle."

"Maybe I can give her some support. I can take leave from work since we aren't that busy."

"There is only one problem, Roger. She doesn't want me to share her whereabouts."

"But I need to know. Don't you understand?"

"Oh, I do," Clarice said with a smug grin.

"You are driving me crazy, Clarice."

"I know. But as you know I have a soft spot for you in my heart and purposely didn't answer Annette with a promise to keep the information from you. So would you like the address of Annette's mom?"

"Stop torturing me. You know very well that I want it."

"Okay," Clarice said and opened the house door.

"Would you like a cup of coffee while I write down the information?"

"Actually, I'm kind of in a hurry. I need to talk to my boss and I need to make travel arrangements."

Clarice only grinned and handed him the paper. "See you around and make sure to fill me in on the developments."

"I owe you, Clarice," Roger said and kissed her on the cheek.

Clarice smiled to herself as Roger rushed out the door. *This man is in love,* she mused. *Go ahead of him, Lord, and take all those barriers out of their way.*

Chapter Twenty-three

Annette opened the door. "What are you doing here?" she asked.

"I had to see you," Roger replied. "I heard that your mom is doing worse and I didn't want you to face the situation by yourself."

Annette started crying, "She isn't doing well at all. The doctor told me that she only has about a week left. I feel so awful. I should have never left her."

Roger held her in his arms. "You are here now and that's what counts." He guided her into the living room and sat down on the couch with her.

Annette sobbed. "Is your Mom awake?" Roger asked.

"No. She is sleeping. But I think she will wake up any moment."

"Honey, who is here?" Annette's mom called from her room.

Annette got up, wiped her face with a wet towel and went to her mom's room. "The young man I told you about."

"Roger, right?"

"That's right Ma'am," Roger answered. *She told her mom about me*, Roger thought to himself as he looked to Annette. Annette blushed.

"I was afraid that she might have called the pastor. I don't need any God, if indeed there is one." Annette and Roger glanced at each other.

"I am not a pastor. But to be honest, I believe in God and want to be a pastor someday."

"Well that's fine and dandy. But if there was truly a God, than He wasn't interested in my life and my misery."

"Life can be very tough sometimes Ma'am, but that doesn't mean that God doesn't care."

"It's easy for you to say. You are hardly old enough to know any hardship."

"I have to disagree with you, Ma'am. My three year-old younger brother drowned when I was only five. I didn't know how to swim yet and had to watch him die."

"Then where was your God when that happened?"

"I asked Him that myself. But over time I learned that He was right there with my brother. I had horrible nightmares about my brother's death until in desperation I cried out to God for help. That night I had the same dream again, except that I saw how Jesus took my brother into His arms and carried him up to the sky. My brother was waving at me and had a peaceful smile on his face."

Annette's Mom was speechless for a moment. "What do we have for dinner?" she asked to divert the conversation.

"I made you some clam chowder, your favorite."

"Thank you, Honey. Will you eat with us, Roger?"

"I would like that very much," Roger replied. He smiled at Annette who blushed again. "Can I help you in the kitchen?" he asked her.

"Of course you can help her," Annette's mom answered. "I'll take the time to rest some more." Her mom's look made Annette blush again.

She went to the kitchen very aware that Roger was right behind her. She could hardly breathe. How would she survive this?

"Can your mom still swallow the clam chowder?"

"Not so well. I need to blend it for her. The doctor said to give her any food she wants as long as it is soft."

"Let me hold the pot for you," Roger offered and brought it closer to the blender. They filled three bowls and went back to the room.

"This tastes great, Honey. You need to know that Annette is quite the cook."

"I believe it. Apparently, Annette and Clarice had lots of practice in their high school years."

"Yes, they did. I willingly tasted everything they made."

Annette's Mom coughed.

"Are you all right?" Annette asked as she went to the bedside and held her mom's hand."

"I am fine. Why don't you two eat in the dining room. I would like to rest some more."

"Okay, Mom," Annette said. When they were in the dining room, Annette cried again. "She is in pain. I know she is trying to hide it, but I keep seeing it in her face."

Roger didn't know what to do. He embraced Annette in a hug and held her tight. It made Annette feel better.

Only a few minutes later Annette's mom called for them again. "Roger, I have another question for you. Why do you suppose that we all have to die? And what will death be like?"

Roger took a seat next to the bed. "Ma'am, it wasn't God's plan for us to die. The reason we have to face death is sin. God's perfect creation is decaying because of sin. But Jesus died once and for all that we might be set free from sin. His intention is for us to live with him forever. Jesus' death has made it possible for us to live even though our body will go back to dust. When we die our soul will be reunited with God if we accept His free gift of salvation."

"Gifts are not free. I learned that the hard way when I received gifts from my uncles who made me 'pay' for them in return."

Roger felt pain for Annette's mom who had endured so much. "God is different. Accepting the gift of salvation is free. It changes us from the inside out and gives us the desire to be close to the Giver and to do His will."

"I know that it changes people. I've seen big changes in Annette since she became a Christian." Pain struck Annette's mom again and she breathed heavily.

Annette was right by her side. "Do you want some pain medicine?"

"No, Honey. They make me sleepy and I have some more questions. I'll be better in a moment."

Annette sat down on the chair next to Roger's. Annette's mom had her eyes closed. Her breathing got easier again and she opened her eyes. "Will you take care of my girl when I'm gone?" she asked Roger.

Roger had not expected this question but willingly replied. "Yes Ma'am, I will."

Annette's face turned red.

"So when people die they will be instantly with God?"

"If they asked for forgiveness for their sins."

Another wave of pain overcame Annette's mom. Annette held her hand and Roger prayed quietly for her mom. When she opened her eyes again she spoke, "I am afraid Roger."

"You can give that fear to Jesus. He will carry you through this difficult time."

"I want to, but I can't approach him. I have sinned so much. There is no way He would listen to me."

"We all have sinned and have fallen short of God's glory. But He promises to take our sins away if we only ask Him."

Annette's mom looked from Roger to Annette. "Can you help me to do so?"

"We would love to," Annette said with tears in her eyes.

"Please repeat after me," Roger said. "Lord I have sinned, please forgive me. I want to be Yours, now and forevermore."

Annette's Mom repeated the prayer. A smile creeped up on her face. "Now I am also one of those crazy Christians."

"Mom, you made me the happiest daughter on this earth. We will spend eternity together." Annette leaned over her mom and gave her a soft kiss on the cheek. Both cried tears of joy. Roger left the room to give them more privacy.

"Come back here, young man," Annette's mom said when she noticed him leaving. "Thank you for your boldness. You saved my life."

"No Ma'am, Jesus did."

"But He used you. You will be a mighty fine pastor. May I ask you to stick around? I would like to have you here when I meet my Lord."

"Yes, Ma'am. I would be honored to be with you for that glorious moment."

Annette gazed at Roger full of thankfulness. "You can sleep in the guest room. I'll call you when we need you."

Roger looked at Annette who had exhaustion written all over her face. "Why don't I stay with your mom tonight and you catch a good night's rest?"

"I think Roger is right, Honey. Rest up."

Annette didn't protest for she was indeed drained. "Thank you," she said and went to her room.

The night was long for Annette's mom. Waves of pain kept coming more frequently. Roger prayed silently and read the Psalms to her. All of a sudden Annette's mom turned to him and said, "It's time. Please get Annette."

Roger knocked on Annette's door and led her to her mom's room.

"Honey, it's time. I will leave you in a moment. I want you to know how much I love you and always have."

"I love you so much, Mom. I don't want to let you go."

"Annette. I am going to a place of peace without pain and sorrow. I remember that my mom told me about it when I was still very little. I am ready to go and I will see my mother, too. Your Grandmother was a very strong Christian." She turned to Roger. "Keep your promise and take care of my girl."

"You don't have to worry. I will take good care of your precious daughter."

"I love you both." With this she closed her eyes. Her breathing stopped. The expression on her face was peaceful and her face glowed.

Annette leaned on Roger's shoulder and just sat there. It seemed like hours had passed. "We need to call the funeral home," Annette said and looked at Roger. "Thank you for being here for me. Knowing that Mom is with the Lord has taken a heavy load off of me. I feel joy in the midst of the pain of losing her."

Roger only smiled. He went with her to the funeral home and made the final arrangements. Annette's mom wanted a very simple and quiet funeral. Annette invited a few friends her mom wanted to attend. When they lowered the casket into the ground sadness overcame Annette and she wept. Roger held her tight and prayed silently for her.

They went back to the house to get it ready to be sold.

"Your mom must have been an order loving lady. Everything is ready and most of it is already packed."

"Yes, my mom loved order. And since she knew that her sickness was fatal, she had me look through all of her belongings and had me choose what I wanted to keep. Most of the rest she gave away. As you can see, she kept the bare minimum, even in the kitchen."

"It seems like your mom has been a strong woman."

"She was. I am glad that I was able to be with her when she fought with the cancer. We had a grand time looking through all her things. She told me a lot about her life that I had not known."

"I am glad you got to spend that time with your mom. I wish I had known her better."

"You would have liked her a lot."

"I liked her from just that little time I had with her."

After a week, the house was ready to go onto the market. Annette gave Roger two boxes, two photo albums and her mom's pepper mill to put into the trunk of his car. "I will think of her when I grind pepper."

Roger smiled at her and packed everything into his car. Annette slept most of the way back to Albuquerque. It was already dark when they arrived at Clarice's house.

"How are you, Annette?" she asked as she embraced her.

"I am all right," she said. "It's good to see you."

"Good to see you too. Come on in. I made a stew for dinner."

"Clarice, you are a jewel. Thanks for the dinner. We haven't taken time to eat a real meal for days," Roger said. They ate and shared about Annette's mom and how she had accepted Christ into her life.

"So what are the plans?" Clarice asked Annette.

"I'll stay in Albuquerque for a while and think about what to do next."

"Please make sure to come by often."

"I will," Annette promised and stretched. "I feel like I could sleep for a week."

"As a matter of fact, I should take you home now. The trip was rather exhausting. Thanks again for dinner."

"You are welcome. I'll see you soon."

Roger dropped off Annette at her mom's friend's house. "I can keep your stuff in my garage until you know what you want to do with it."

"Thank you, Roger. I think that's a great idea. But the pepper mill comes with me today."

Roger smiled at Annette. "Here it is. I'll call you tomorrow to see how you are."

"Thanks for everything. I don't know how I could have done it without you."

"It was my pleasure. Sleep well."

Annette went to bed and fell asleep immediately.

Roger drove home deep in thought. *I really love her Lord. She is so special. Help me to help her through this tough time. Be with her and comfort her,* he prayed. *I would like to date her, but she will need some time to mourn her mother's death. Help me to be patient.*

His house felt lonelier than ever before. He wanted Annette here with him, in his arms. Was this how Jacob from the Bible felt when he waited for Rachel all those years? It surely wouldn't take that long, would it?

Chapter Twenty-four

"How are you feeling?" Clarice asked Annette after they sat down in the living room with a cup of coffee.

"I miss Mom a lot. But I also feel such peace. To know that Mom is with the Lord makes me happy in the midst of my pain."

"I can't tell you how happy I am for you. I prayed for your mom's salvation ever since you told me that she was so opposed to God."

"Your prayers were answered," Annette smiled.

"I wasn't the only one praying. I know you prayed, and Roger prayed of course, too," Clarice said with a grin on her face. "So how are things between you two?"

"Roger is wonderful. He was very supportive. I don't know what I would have done without him."

"So when are you guys going to date officially?" Clarice asked with an innocent look on her face.

"Clarice. I thought about it long and hard. I truly love him. That's why I have to go. As a matter of fact I am leaving this afternoon."

Clarice was speechless for a while and stared at Annette. "You can't mean that."

"There is no other way."

"But where will you go?"

"I can't tell you. But I will be in contact, I promise."

"Annette, this man is in love with you. I have never seen him this way. You will break his heart."

"He will get over it. He deserves better."

"But Annette …"

"Please stop. I made up my mind. I don't want Roger to suffer because of my past. He deserves a woman who is pure."

Clarice wanted to protest but Annette lifted her hand. "Nothing can change my mind. I have to go now and get ready. Thank you for everything. Please say hi to the kids."

Clarice couldn't find any words. They embraced for a long hug. "I will miss you," Clarice said as a tear ran down her face. "You are like a sister I never had."

"I feel the same about you. Goodbye Clarice." They embraced again.

Clarice closed the door behind Annette and sat down at the table. *This can't be it*, she thought. *They love each other. This simply can't be.* Clarice sat motionless for a while. Then a smile formed slowly on her face. She picked up the phone and dialed. "Hey it's Roger. Please leave me a message."

"Roger. It's Clarice. Call me. It's very important." Clarice put the phone down. *Why isn't he picking up the phone? I need to talk to him. Lord, help me. It can't end like this. They are both in love. I can't let her walk away from this man.*

Clarice picked up the phone. The doorbell rang when she started dialing. She went to answer the door. "Roger!" she exclaimed as she hugged him.

"How are you?"

"You need to pursue Annette. You have to go right now."

"Clarice. She just lost her mom. This is hardly the time to move forward in my relationship with Annette."

"She is leaving and this time she is not sharing her whereabouts with me."

"But why?" Roger said in bewilderment.

"You will have to find out for yourself."

Roger turned and ran out the door. He drove to Annette's place. When he rang the doorbell there was no answer but he saw movements through the window. He knocked on the door and opened it. He went in and strode to where Annette was standing with a small suitcase in her hand. *I forgot to lock the door*, Annette thought to herself.

"Annette," Roger said as he hugged her tight. "You can't leave. You belong to me."

"It can't be," Annette said, fighting tears.

"But why? I love you."

"You don't know me and don't know anything about my past. You deserve better."

"Believe me, there is nothing that can separate us. I want you in my life. It doesn't matter what happened in the past."

Annette held onto Roger as tears ran down her cheeks. Roger kissed her forehead. "I love you. Nothing can change that."

"I love you, too," Annette said.

Roger led her to the sofa. "Why don't you tell me what tortures you so much?" he asked softly.

Annette considered his suggestion. She felt peace and security in his presence. "Clarice and I had been best friends since pre-school," she began. "We were closer than sisters, spending every possible minute together. We shared secrets; I borrowed Clarice's dresses and lent her mine. We could even finish each other's sentences. That was until high school. Then things changed. Paul joined our school in his junior year. Clarice and I had major crushes on him; but he only had eyes for Clarice. They started to go out together. Clarice even invited me to come along. But I didn't go. I was jealous. Why did he have to choose her instead of me? And why would she let him come between us?

"I decided I would break up their relationship and become his girlfriend. Well, I was successful. Paul and Clarice broke up and Paul started dating me. I felt victorious and went along with everything Paul wanted. I ended up pregnant. Of course I was excited and told Paul the good news that very night. But instead of sharing my joy he got mad. He started throwing things and threatened to dump me if I didn't abort the baby." Annette sobbed. "I was afraid to lose Paul. I had to take care of things right away before I would change my mind. I went to a clinic the next day and had them …" Annette's body shook from her crying. Roger held her close and rocked her.

When Annette calmed she went on. "I wasn't supposed to see anything, but I did see what they had removed. There were little hands and feet and I realized what I had done. I felt cold and empty inside and cried silently. A kind nurse held me for what seemed to be hours. When I went to see

Paul he was still in a bad mood. I was so sad I couldn't even talk. He started yelling at me and asked if I had taken care of the problem. I only nodded. He wanted me to go to bed with him but I was hurting physically and emotionally. He threw me out that very night. I spent the night in a park hidden under a bush.

I longed to talk to Clarice. But after all I had done I just knew she wouldn't forgive me. So I went home to my mom's when she was at work and freshened up. I decided to put on a normal face. The abortion would be my own little secret. I told Mom that I had broken up with Paul and stayed with her until my graduation. After that, Mom moved to Denver, Colorado, for a better job, and I moved to California to start over. But my guilt and shame followed me there and they are still haunting me today."

Roger took Annette's hands into his own. "What happened in the past is in the past. With Jesus you have a new life. Let go of the old life. You are a new creation. Your sins are gone and forgiven. They are as far as the east is from the west. God doesn't hold them against you and I don't either."

Annette sobbed. Roger took her into his arms. "I love you, Annette, and nothing can change that."

Annette felt the heaviness of the past lift off her shoulders. She leaned into him and wished that this moment would never pass. She felt his comforting warmth, his strong chest and arms and smelled the fragrance of his aftershave. She now knew for sure that she could share a life with this wonderful man. It wasn't a forbidden dream anymore, separated by the sins of the past, but a gift from God, so pure and lovely that she could never have imagined it.

"I love you, Roger," Annette whispered.

Roger lifted her face. "I love you so much," he said tenderly and kissed her. It was a kiss of love and acceptance, with a hint of desire. Breathless, Roger pulled away. Desire for Annette was written all over his face. "I better go now," he said with a hoarse voice.

Annette understood, for her body ached with desire for Roger as well. "I'll see you tomorrow," Roger said as he squeezed her hands.

"See you tomorrow," Annette whispered. She couldn't move from where she sat. Her heart was racing still remembering the time she spent with Roger. She knew that they couldn't meet privately like this anymore. Both of their desires were too strong to withstand the temptation of becoming one.

When Annette finally went to bed she could hardly fall asleep. Full of joy and thankfulness she prayed. God was so good to her. Mom died knowing salvation and Roger loved her so much that her past didn't destroy that love. *Lord, You truly turn everything for good. Your promises are true.*

Chapter Twenty-five

Roger couldn't sleep. He lay in bed and reflected on the last month. He could hardly believe the blessings God had bestowed on him. Clarice was right. God had a very special wife planned for him. Annette was kind and tenderhearted. She loved children and most of all loved God. They would be able to walk together in life, serving God.

Roger knew his calling was to be a pastor and he couldn't think of a better person to stand by his side and minister together with him than Annette.

Roger was off from work the next day. Sleep never claimed him; he took a long hot shower and drank some strong coffee before he reached for the phone.

"Hello," he heard Clarice's sleepy voice.

"You've got to help me!" Roger said.

"Are you okay? Did somebody get hurt? Is your mom alright?" Clarice asked as she jumped out of bed.

"Everything is fine," Roger chuckled. "I just need for you to find out what Annette's ring size is."

Clarice stood frozen. The words finally sank in. "You mean for an engagement ring?" she almost screamed.

"What do you know? My friend catches on even early in the morning."

"Easy for you to say," Clarice said. "The cat kept me up almost all night."

"Then you're forgiven," he teased, not willing to share that he was up all night too, thinking about Annette. "When can you find out?"

"I have to wait for her to call me. And I am sure that she will call, because she has some news she will want to share with me," Clarice said with a smug smile. "I'll invite her to lunch and take her shopping afterward."

"But don't make it obvious. I want it to be a surprise," Roger said.

"She won't even know. Fiona has her birthday coming up. We'll look for some rings for Fiona and try some on ourselves just for fun. When do you want the information?"

"As soon as you can call me. I'll have my phone with me."

"Okay. I'll talk to you soon."

"Bye and thanks, Clarice."

"My pleasure," Clarice said delighted.

Chapter Twenty-six

Clarice walked into Giuseppe's. She saw Annette at a table with a dreamy look on her face. *Thank you Lord for answering my prayer for Annette and Roger.*

Clarice came to the table and Annette beamed at her. "He loves me, even with the stain of my past."

"I told you. Roger is an incredible guy."

"I know," Annette smiled. "I don't deserve such happiness. God is so good to me."

Clarice squeezed Annette's hand. "I can't tell you how delighted I am for you two." She picked up the menu. "Have you ordered yet?"

"I am not hungry. I'll just have a cup of coffee."

"I am starved." Clarice ordered a sandwich and a soda.

"I wish Mom could have known him more. She would have liked him a lot. She asked Roger many questions about God. I almost fainted when she asked him to take care of me."

"She must have sensed your attraction for each other. Mothers usually have a hunch when their girls are in love."

"I guess so. She wanted him to be with us when she met the Lord. I am so glad that he showed up. I don't know if Mom would have accepted Christ into her heart otherwise. It all happened so fast. I still can't believe that Mom died that very night. I miss her so much but I am happy and relieved to know that she is in heaven." Annette took a sip of her coffee. "Is it terrible of me to be in love even though I just lost my mother?" she asked Clarice.

"I don't think so, Annette. Besides, she is with Jesus now. There will come days when the pain of your loss will seem to be unbearable. But Roger will help you to overcome it."

Annette had that dreamy look again. Clarice finished her sandwich and asked, "Can you come with me to find a birthday present for Fiona? She wants jewelry and I know just the place where they might carry what she likes."

"Of course I'll come with you. I don't have any other plans."

They grabbed their purses and went to the mall. "This store might have what I am looking for. See these rings right here? I think she'll like them."

"I think so, too. Oh look at these. I like these even better." Annette slid one of them on her finger. "This one is beautiful."

"Can I try it, too?" Clarice asked as Annette took the ring off her finger. "You have much finer fingers than me. Look it barely fits on my pinky."

"Too bad that I didn't bring my credit card. I really like it."

"I tell you what, Annette. Your birthday is coming up and I'll buy it for you if you promise to forget how it looks."

"I can't promise that," Annette laughed, "but I like the idea."

"Okay. It's a deal. And I'll take this one for Fiona. She likes pink and she'll love the butterfly design on it." Clarice paid for both and turned back to Annette. "Do you want to come to my house?"

"I actually need to go home. Roger will call me after work and I don't want to miss his call."

"All right. I can give you a ride."

"That would be nice."

Clarice dropped off Annette and went home. She picked up the phone and called Roger. "Hi, it's Clarice. You may want to come by after work today. I have something for you."

"Did you get Annette's ring size?"

"No. But I bought her a ring that she liked. You can take it along when you hunt for her engagement ring."

"I will be there in about ten minutes."

Clarice smiled. A few minutes later the doorbell rang. "Come on in, Roger. Here is the ring."

Roger stayed in the doorway. "Thank you, Clarice. You are such a pal. I'd better get going right away."

Clarice closed the door behind Roger. Her friends were in love. She was happy for them, but felt a little sadness when Quinn came to her mind. *Lord, I still love him so much. Please work a miracle for us. I can't do anything to fix our situation. But You are more than able. I praise You, oh Lord.*

Clarice fixed herself a cup of tea and sat down with her Bible. About an hour later Lisa and Isabelle stormed into the house. "Mom, can we make pudding?"

"That's a great idea. I didn't make any dessert for after dinner yet."

"Where is the recipe?" Lisa asked.

"In the drawer. Do you want chocolate or vanilla?"

"I want chocolate," Isabelle said.

"I'd rather have vanilla," Lisa declared.

"How about both. Then we can have some for tomorrow too. Isabelle, you make the chocolate one, and Lisa you make the vanilla pudding."

When they were finished Clarice said, "Okay girls. Now it's time to do your homework. We will have dinner in an hour."

"Okay Mom," the girls said and sat down at the table with their school books.

"I don't like math," Isabelle said. "We have to do ten problems."

"I wish I had to do math instead of the science paper," Lisa replied.

"Why don't we switch?" Isabelle suggested.

"No way," Clarice said who had overheard their discussion. "Your homework is to help you practice what you learned."

The girls sighed and got started. "Are you done?" Clarice asked when dinner was ready.

"I have to finish one more paragraph," Lisa said.

"You can have five more minutes," Clarice told her. "Isabelle, where are you?"

"I'm in my room."

"Are you finished?" Clarice asked.

"Yes, Mom. It was easy," Isabelle said.

"Then you can help me set the table. We'll eat in the kitchen today."

"Can I use the Cinderella plate tonight?"

"Yes. And Lisa can have the Snow White plate. Please put a plate for Fiona on the table as well. She will be home any moment now."

"What about Norbert?" Isabelle asked.

"He is at the movies with his friends."

"That's not fair. It's a school night and I never get to go anywhere on school nights." Isabelle complained.

"He is older than you, Honey. Don't worry. Your time will come soon enough."

"It's just not fair."

"Life isn't always fair."

"But Mom…"

"One more word and you will stand in the corner."

Isabelle went quiet but the look on her face showed that she was still upset. "Time to eat," she announced when the table was ready.

"I am not finished with my homework yet," Lisa complained.

"You can do it after we eat. Come on. We don't want dinner to get cold," Clarice said.

They were starting to eat their dessert when the doorbell rang. Annette and Roger stood in front of the door. "Come on in," Clarice said. "We just started our dessert. Would you like some?"

"We only have a moment," Annette smiled. "I just wanted you to see something." Annette showed Clarice her left hand, decorated with a beautiful diamond ring on her ring finger.

"You got engaged?" Clarice screamed and hugged Annette. "I am so happy for you two." She hugged Roger.

Lisa and Isabelle ran into the hallway. "What is going on," they wanted to know.

"Uncle Roger and Annette are engaged," Clarice told them.

"That's great. When will you get married?" they wanted to know.

"Soon," Roger answered with a big smile.

"Can we carry the flowers?" Isabelle asked.

"I couldn't think of anyone more fitting for the honors," Annette said excitedly.

"Mom, we will have to look for nice dresses. Can we go tomorrow?" Lisa asked.

"Slow down young lady. It all depends when Annette and Uncle Roger want to have their wedding."

"We decided to have it in September," Annette said with a dreamy look.

"You two move pretty fast, don't you?" Clarice teased.

"We both have a witness in our spirit that it is God's will for us to be married. So there is no reason for us to wait," Roger said with sincerity in his voice.

"I am convinced that you both belong together," Clarice said with a twinkle in her eye.

"Sorry to cut this visit short, Clarice. But Annette and I need to go now."

"I understand. Thanks for letting me know this wonderful news. I love you both."

"Bye," the girls chimed and went back to their desserts.

"We love you too; you and your entire family," Annette said and embraced Clarice. They left the house.

"I guess we can start shopping for dresses for the two of you this weekend."

"That will be so much fun, Mom," Lisa smiled.

"I want a blue dress," Isabelle declared.

"The color depends on what Annette chooses."

"Can we call her and find out?" Isabelle wanted to know.

"That will have to wait. Uncle Roger and Annette have things to do right now. I will call her tomorrow and ask her."

"I can't wait to find a dress. I want to look like a princess."

Clarice smiled. "You are my little princesses, both of you. And we will find the perfect gown for you."

Fiona came in minutes later.

"You missed it," Lisa said. "Uncle Roger and Annette are getting married."

"And we will be flower girls," Isabelle said proudly.

"So I was right," Fiona grinned. "When is the big day?"

"In September."

"Too bad. I will be overseas by then." Fiona had decided to go as an exchange student overseas for this coming school year.

"We will take lots of photos for you. Then you can look at them when you return."

"It's not the same as being there, but better than nothing."

Norbert walked in the door.

"You missed dinner," Clarice greeted him.

"I'm not hungry."

"Where were you? I thought you went to the early show."

"None of your business," Norbert snapped and went to his room.

Lord, what can I do with this son of mine? What am I doing wrong? Help me; give me Your wisdom to deal with this situation.

"Time to get ready for bed," Clarice told Lisa and Isabelle.

They were excited and made all kinds of plans for accessories and shoes and purses, while they readied for bed. Clarice enjoyed their excitement. *Lord I feel so blessed with these beautiful girls. Thank you so much for them.*

When bed time finally came Clarice lay awake for a long time. She thought of her own wedding. It had been one of the most precious days of her entire life. *Oh Lord, my heart hurts over our situation. I trust that You are in control and that You have a perfect plan. Bless Quinn right now. Let him know how much You love him. Heal all his hurts and fill him with Your peace.*

Clarice fell asleep, dreaming of a "happy ever after."

Chapter Twenty-seven

"I am sorry, Lydia, that I am not good company today. Maybe it would have been better to reschedule our lunch date."

"What's the matter, Clarice? What makes your heart so heavy?"

"I keep thinking of Quinn's affair. It seems to consume me today. I feel unable to do anything at all."

"I understand, Clarice. It hurts deeply and you feel like you have been replaced. You ask yourself if you are not pretty enough, thin enough, big enough, loving enough. Basically you feel like you are not enough."

Clarice stared at Lydia. "That's kind of how I feel. How do you know? Did Tom have an affair?"

"Yes. About ten years ago."

"I am so sorry, Lydia. How did you deal with this?"

"When I found out about his affair I was devastated. I quit my job and ran away. I left a letter for Tom explaining that I found out about the other woman and that I would come to pack up my stuff when I was ready. I had saved some money every month to buy Tom a boat on our 25th wedding anniversary. He always wanted one. I withdrew the money from savings and just drove to the highway and then continued driving aimlessly. After driving all night, I was too exhausted to go any further. I looked for a place to stay but couldn't find anything. So I waited till morning. The town I had come to was small. There were a few houses, a grocery store, a little church and fields everywhere you turned. I went to the grocery store. The few people I met on the street tried to avoid me. One woman even turned around and went back to her house. It was weird. But I was too drained to fully notice. When I asked the grocery clerk about a hotel, he was very short and unfriendly. 'We don't need any strangers here,' he said. Even here I was unwanted. When I turned to leave, a friendly lady touched my arm. 'Don't mind him,' she said. 'You can stay with my family. Come, I'll show you where we live.'

"I followed her. She went to a little house next to the church. 'Come on in and meet my husband and children.'"

"Was he the pastor, since their house was right by the church?"

"You guessed right. He was just as friendly as his wife. And the children, five of them, were lively and sweet. Lori, that's the woman's name, showed me to their guest room. It was small but at the same time comfortable and bright. It even had its own little bathroom. After washing my face I rested on the bed. Before I knew it I was fast asleep. I slept all day but woke up exhausted. I sat up, my head pounding. Bad memories came up without warning. I suspected that Tom had had an affair, but had pushed those thoughts away. I even met her. Tom had brought her to dinner. I convinced myself that it was innocent. She was just a co-worker. But my instincts had been right. He had spoken her name in his sleep. I still thought of it as innocent. But when I found a letter from her with a not-so-innocent picture of her inside, my suspicions had been confirmed. I have to admit that those memories still come up at times and try to pull me down."

"How were you able to overcome this hurt? How could you ever trust Tom again?"

"It took me quite some time. I stayed with the pastor's family for about three months. They never asked what was wrong. But after a few weeks, I confided my troubles to Lori and Peter, her husband. My faith and their loving counsel helped me over the worst. A week before I went back home, I surrendered my hurt to God. I made a firm resolution to keep my eyes on Christ and leave my future in His hands. I came to love Lori, Peter and their children and saying goodbye was hard. I went back home, not knowing what to expect. My greatest fear was to find the other woman moved into our home.

"I arrived on a Tuesday midday. Not much had changed in our home. I prayerfully packed my things. While I was packing I found notes everywhere. They read: please stay with me; please forgive me; I still love you. In my insecurity I thought these notes must have been for the other woman. I was just about done packing when I heard the door open. Tom came in.

"He looked pale and thin. I picked up one of my bags to put it into the car but Tom spoke up in a broken voice. 'Lydia,' he said, 'please forgive me. I know I am not worthy to ask you to stay with me. You deserve better. I have acted horribly and hurt you deeply. I still love you but I can't expect you to love me back after what I have done to you.'

"For the first time in my life I saw Tom crying. I couldn't move. I just felt numb. I dropped my bags and sat down on the sofa sobbing. This was our chance to reconcile and I almost let it pass by. It took us several months of working through our problems but we were able to keep our marriage together."

"I hope you don't mind me asking, but were you able to be intimate with Tom again?"

"I don't mind you asking. It actually took a long time before we were physically intimate again. Tom slept many nights on the sofa. This gave us a chance to really become friends. It was not based on the physical anymore. Tom started to respect me in a deeper way and our relationship became stronger each day. Our physical intimacy became a true expression of our love and respect for one another."

"But your relationship must be weaker now than before the affair."

"Strangely it is stronger now than ever. We both have learned to love unconditionally on a different level."

"But how can you be so close to him after he has chosen another woman over you?"

"It is called forgiveness. I believe that Satan has tried to destroy my marriage. But through forgiveness we have become stronger than I ever could've thought possible. And what Satan had planned for evil, God has turned to good. We are actively helping other couples who deal with unfaithfulness. God has performed many miraculous healings of relationships before our eyes."

Clarice sat quietly. "So there is still hope for Quinn and me?" she said softly as tears filled her eyes.

"Yes there is."

Both women sat in silence for many more moments before Clarice had to go back home.

Chapter Twenty-eight

The doorbell rang.

"Come on in. The door is unlocked," Clarice hollered.

"Hi, Clarice," Lydia said as she stepped inside and made her way to the kitchen. "Sorry I'm so late. The traffic was horrible."

"That's all right. I'm running behind too. We overslept and the girls are getting ready right now. Fiona and Norbert just left a few minutes ago."

"Is there anything I can help you with?"

"Yes. Please pour some milk into the traveling cups that are sitting on the table."

"Mom, I can't find my backpack," Isabelle yelled from her bedroom.

"Look by the front door. I think you left it there yesterday after school."

Isabelle ran to the front door. "Got it. Thanks."

"I need a signature on my permission slip and five dollars for our class trip to the museum," Lisa said waiving a paper in her hand.

"Bring me a pen Lisa and I'll sign it. There are five dollars in my purse in the front pocket."

"Found it. Oh, hi, Miss Lydia."

"Hi, Lisa."

"Take a granola bar and an apple for you and your sister. I'm almost finished with your lunches."

"Let me finish them, so you can fill out the permission slip," Lydia offered.

"Thanks," Clarice wiped her hands on the kitchen towel and took care of the papers.

"Are you two ready?" Clarice asked.

"Yes," Lisa said and shoved the papers into her backpack.

"Turn off the lights in the bathroom and let's go," Clarice said as she pulled her car keys out of their designated purse pocket. "Would you care to join us, Lydia?"

"Of course," Lydia replied and they all rushed to the car and made their way to the school.

"I have to sign them in," Clarice told Lydia and disappeared with the girls in the school building.

When Clarice came back, Lydia had a wide grin on her face, "I caught you on one of your famous extreme rush days again."

"Yup," Clarice said with a weak smile. "Let's go back to the house. I could use a cup of tea right now."

"Sounds good," Lydia replied.

Back at the house, Clarice brewed a pot of tea and pulled out the waffles from the day before. "Would you care for a waffle?" she asked Lydia. "They taste great toasted."

"Yes. Do you have some of your special syrup to go with it?"

"Of course."

A few minutes later both sat at the kitchen table, a plate with waffles and a steaming cup of tea in front of them.

"This tastes delicious. You should have become a chef, Clarice."

"I actually thought about it, but I never pursued it. It's a very stressful work, I was told."

"If anyone can handle stress, it's you Clarice."

"For a short time yes. But I don't know if I could do this all day long. For right now I enjoy cooking and baking for our needs. So, how are things going?"

"Pretty good. The only thing is that Tom has an infected tooth and needs a root canal. But instead of getting it over with he just keeps rescheduling his appointments."

"I don't blame him. It sounds like a painful procedure is awaiting him."

"He's tried avoiding the dentist ever since he was a little boy." Lydia sipped her tea. "Isn't it weird how we all struggle with different issues and put them off, hoping they'll go away on their own somehow?"

"Yes. Until they turn into bigger issues. I had a bill due a week ago and waited too long. Now I have to pay an extra fee and feel pretty guilty to have wasted my money by not paying it right away."

"Those things bug me too when they happen. I want to be wise with my resources. Procrastination and I know each other too well," Lydia said with a comical expression.

Clarice laughed, "You could be a comedian with all your different expressions."

Lydia joined her laughter.

"So how are Annette and Roger? They always leave right after church. I haven't talked to them since their engagement."

"They are fine. I don't see too much of them lately," Clarice smiled. "They have too many things on their mind with planning for their wedding and honeymoon."

"I was taken by surprise when Annette told me that their wedding will be in September. They kind of move a little fast I think."

"Normally I would agree. But knowing them both, I am confident that they are meant to be married to each other. Roger shared with me that he has a witness in his spirit that God planned for Annette to be his wife. I know that Roger's heart is after God and that he doesn't take marriage lightly."

"I sure am excited for them. They are very special people."

"I would have played match maker if necessary but I didn't even have to," Clarice said with a grin.

"I could see you practically pushing them into each other's arms. On another note, how are things with Quinn?" she asked.

"I haven't seen him since last week. He is really busy with work. I sometimes wonder if he has another girlfriend."

"Has he asked for a divorce again?"

"No. I don't know how this all can work out. I keep hearing that song on the radio that proclaims that 'God can heal this home'. But I wonder if that applies to mine too."

"Clarice, if anyone knows that God can do anything it is you. Remember all the times when God came through for you. I truly have a witness in my heart that God will heal your marriage and your family. Hold on to what you know of your God. He is great and mighty to save."

"Sometimes He chooses not to heal a marriage."

"I know. But He wouldn't have given you those visions and words."

"That's true. I just don't know how this all can turn around. The worst part is that I at times get so frustrated and angry with Quinn and say things to him that hurt his feelings."

"That happens to everyone."

"But with me it happens in front of the kids. It makes me feel terrible because I disrespect him in front of them."

"Have you prayed about this?"

"Yes. I even apologized to Quinn. I don't know why I get so mad at him."

"There is probably hurt from the past in you that you have to let go of. Just keep praying about it. The Lord will help you."

"Thanks. I'll do that." Clarice fell quiet.

Lydia waited, knowing that something else was on Clarice's heart. Tears ran down Clarice's cheeks.

"Lydia, I have a thought on my mind that wants to bring me down." Clarice paused and started to speak again, "What if Quinn has a STD? I know he had physical relations with at least one other woman since we separated. But what if he picked up a disease. And when God restores my marriage, how do I confront him about this without hurting him?"

Lydia looked at her friend with empathy, "I know how you feel. I had the same thoughts about Tom after his affair."

"What did you do?"

"I asked him to be tested before I was physically intimate with him again. It was hard to ask him but I couldn't let him come close to me without assurance that he wasn't infected."

"Was he upset with you?"

"Yes. He actually disappeared for a week. But he finally worked through it. He apologized and went to be tested. Being unfaithful has its consequences."

"Do you ever wonder if he still thinks about the other woman?"

"Ever so often. But I keep praying for inner healing for myself. I don't want to be controlled by this thought."

Clarice sighed. "Why does life have to be so difficult at times?"

"We wouldn't need God if everything was easy."

"I guess you're right. I am very close to Him because He has shown Himself faithful in all my difficult situations. I have learned to depend on Him and have come to realize that I truly need Him in my life."

"I can't live without God anymore either."

"Would you like another cup of tea?"

"No, thank you. I have to go now."

"See you on Sunday then."

"Yes. Bye Clarice and thanks for the delicious waffles."

"You are welcome."

Clarice cleaned the dishes and started dinner. Norbert was on her mind. *Lord, I don't know what to do anymore. I can't let Norbert treat me and the girls disrespectfully like this anymore. I wish I could have Quinn on my side to fight this battle. But I disagree with Quinn's way of controlling us by making us feel bad and by demeaning us. I sense that Lisa and Isabelle, though they love their brother, are somewhat afraid of Norbert. It shouldn't be like this. I love all my children. What can I do, oh Lord, to make this work?*

The phone rang. "Hello."

"Hi. I am Norbert's math teacher. I need to inform you that Norbert hasn't attended my class for the last three days."

"But he told me yesterday that he took a math test and will have a good grade on it."

"I am sorry to inform you that he lied to you. We had a test but Norbert wasn't present to take the test. I heard from two of my colleagues that Norbert hasn't shown up for their classes either."

"I am sorry. I'll talk to Norbert when he gets home."

"You should also know that Norbert hasn't done any of his homework for a month now. I sent you a few letters but you never responded."

"I am sorry but I never received the letters. I will confront Norbert about that as well."

"Thank you. And feel free to call me if you have any questions."

"I will."

Clarice hung up the phone. *He hasn't been to school? How could I have missed that. And what has he been doing in all that time?*

Clarice felt unable to move. The door opened and Fiona and Norbert came in arguing with each other. "You are so stupid," Norbert said to Fiona.

"That's enough. If you can't say anything nice you don't say anything at all," Clarice cut in.

"Oh shut up, Mom," Norbert said defiantly.

"Go to your room. You may come back when you are ready to apologize to me."

"You can't tell me what to do."

"Here we go again," Fiona said and made her way to her room.

"I had a phone call from your teacher. She says that you haven't attended her class as well as your other classes. What have you been doing?" Clarice asked, trying to keep her voice calm.

"None of your business," Norbert muttered.

"It is my business. If you are not going to school you need to find a job and move out."

"Oh just shut up, you idiot."

"Go to your room right now before I lose my patience."

"Get a life, Mom," Norbert said and went to his room.

Lord what can I do? This is totally out of hand.

Clarice was glad that Lisa and Isabelle walked home from school today. She didn't feel up to driving the car right now. She concentrated on dinner when Norbert stood in front of her with two back packs in his hands. "I am leaving. You won't ever see me again." He stomped out the door.

Clarice decided to let him walk off. He would be back by evening. She used to be totally upset in the past when Norbert would threaten to leave. But he had always returned home.

"Lisa, please set the table. Dinner will be ready in ten minutes."

"Where is Norbert?" Lisa asked when they all sat down to eat.

"I don't know. But I am sure he will show up soon."

The girls had gone to bed and Norbert had not yet come home. Clarice started to get worried. She lay down on the sofa to wait up for Norbert only to wake up in the morning realizing that Norbert still wasn't home.

Clarice picked up the phone. "Quinn, Norbert didn't come home last night. Do you know where he might be?"

"No."

"Maybe I should call the police."

"I'll do it. Let an adult handle this."

Clarice hung up the phone in anger. Why did she even talk to him about her problems? Quinn would only use them against her. Maybe Norbert would come back this evening. She woke the girls and sent them off to school.

When she was by herself she called Lydia. "Do you have a moment?"

"About five minutes. I have to go to a meeting that I can't miss."

"Then I'll make this fast. Norbert ran away from home yesterday. His teacher called me and told me that Norbert had missed school the last three days. I threatened that he would have to find a job if he wasn't willing to go to school. So he packed up some stuff and left. I didn't go after him because I thought he would be back by evening. But he hasn't returned."

"Have you called the police?"

"No, Quinn is doing it. He said that an 'adult' should take care of it."

"Quinn makes me angry. You need his support, not this."

"I know. He probably thinks it is all my fault."

"Don't believe it. Norbert has made some bad choices lately. You can only do so much."

"Oh, Lydia. I feel totally defeated."

"I wish I had more time. I will pray for you, and tonight Tom and I will pray together."

"Thank you, Lydia. Talk to you soon."

Tears ran down Clarice's face. *Lord, I would like for You to take me home. I am at the end of my rope. I feel like such a failure. I feel like I am playing a game without instructions and that's why I keep failing in my attempts to discipline the children. And it seems there is no one who can help me, except You alone.*

So here I am. HELP!!! Or take me out of this game.

Chapter Twenty-nine

A month had passed with no sign of Norbert. Clarice managed as well as she could on a day-to-day, even minute-to-minute basis. Lisa and Isabelle missed their big brother. "He can be mean at times, but I miss him terribly," Lisa confided to Clarice.

That night Isabelle came to Clarice's bedroom. "Mommy, I need to talk to you."

"Hop on my bed, Isabelle," Clarice said as she closed her Bible. "What's going on?"

"I hurt so much."

"Did you fall down that hard at school?"

"No, I mean yes. That still hurts a little, too."

"So tell me what else hurts."

"Inside. Mommy, it hurts that our family is broken, that all these things are happening."

"What things?"

"You and Dad are separated, and Norbert ran away, and everything is falling apart."

"I am sorry, Honey, that you are hurting so much. To be honest, I am hurting too. But we have a God to run to."

"What if I give up, Mommy?"

"What do you mean?"

"I don't know if I can believe in God anymore. He hasn't done anything and I have prayed so much."

"Honey, God is always working, even if we don't see it. And He is not a wishing well who fulfills all of our wishes and requests. But He uses everything that happens to us for our good as the scripture says in Romans 8:28, *All things work together for good to them that love God and are called according to His purpose."*

"But Mommy, it hurts so bad."

Clarice pulled Isabelle close. "I know, Honey, and I am sorry you feel that deep hurt. I am hurting too but the wonderful thing is that although I am hurting I have unspeakable joy in my heart. I have the assurance that God is right there with me. He knows what I am going through and He carries me through."

"But it hurts so much. At school I just start crying and nobody understands."

"God understands and He is right there with you."

"I don't think He understands. I don't know if I can believe anymore."

"Isabelle, when things get hard you only have two choices. Either you do what many others do and drown your hurt with alcohol, drugs, and so many other things. That will only numb the pain for a short time. Or you go to God with it. You tell Him how much you hurt and ask Him for His help. Things may not change, but God will see you through. You will experience His love and peace and joy in the midst of your hurt. I know that from experience. I have gone through extremely hard times in my life, but God has always been there with me. In the midst of all my pain I felt God's peace, love and joy. It really, really hurts me that our family is torn apart. And it rips me apart that I don't know where Norbert is. But I know beyond the shadow of a doubt that God is with me and that He will turn everything to good that Satan means for evil. I can't promise that our family will be healed, although that is my greatest wish. But I know that I can trust God, because He has a purpose for all of us."

"But I don't know if I can do that. I don't know if I can trust God anymore."

"I encourage you to trust Him and I will be praying for you. I love you, Honey."

"I love you too, Mommy."

"I think it's time to sleep. You can stay in my bed if you like."

"I would like that. Good night, Mom."

"Good night, Isabelle."

Chapter Thirty

Clarice and Annette were in the back room of the church, putting on their gowns. Clarice secured the veil in Annette's hair and stepped back. "You look lovely, Annette. Roger will faint when he sees you."

"Hopefully not," Annette grinned. "I don't want to postpone the wedding." Annette picked up her flowers. "I am so happy, I could cry."

Clarice just smiled. Both women took a last look in the mirror. "Thank you for letting me be your maid of honor. I can't express what that means to me. You and Roger are my closest friends."

"Clarice, you are my dearest friend. I couldn't have thought of anyone else to fill this place on this special day for Roger and me."

There was a knock at the door. "It's time," Lydia said.

Clarice and Annette exited the room. "Thank you for getting Lisa and Isabelle ready for me, Lydia."

"You are welcome."

Clarice walked down the aisle on the arm of Roger's friend Frank from college, his best man. They found their places by the altar. Lisa and Isabelle followed, dropping rose petals to the floor.

Then it was Annette's turn. She walked gracefully down the aisle. Roger couldn't take his eyes off his bride and gladly took her hand when she was by his side. Clarice couldn't help the tears of joy running down her cheeks.

The service was wonderful. Pastor talked about Jesus as the foundation for marriage. "Keep your eyes on the Lord and in everything, be it joy, pain, or difficulty; come together in prayer before Him. He will be there to strengthen you and to guide you. His ways are perfect and we are made perfect in Him."

The service ended with the song "Jesus is our Rock and our Foundation."

"It is the wish of Roger and Annette, to have you all stay and celebrate with them. The reception will take place in the meeting room."

Roger, Annette, Frank and Clarice sat down at the head table. The room had been transformed into a ballroom with blue and white decorations everywhere. Roger started the celebration with prayer. "Dear Lord, thank you for this wonderful day. Thank you for my beautiful wife. Bless all who are gathered here and let this celebration bring You glory. Bless this food and all the lovely people who prepared it for us. In Jesus' name we pray. Amen." Roger took Annette by the hand. "Come my precious bride, let's have something to eat." Clarice and Frank helped themselves to food as well. The evening was lovely. Roger opened the dancing with Annette.

They are so beautiful together. Bless them abundantly oh Lord and protect their marriage. Clarice thought of her own wedding and how deep in love she had been. *Oh Lord, please restore my marriage. I still love Quinn so much. There is no other man who could ever take Quinn's place.* Clarice couldn't help the feeling of sadness that overcame her. She went outside to get some fresh air.

Annette had seen the expression on Clarice's face. When the dance was over she said, "Roger, can you please talk to Clarice. She seems very sad."

"I noticed, too. Maybe it would be better if you talk to her, Annette."

"Okay, I will."

Annette found Clarice outside "Are you all right?"

"Not really. I thought of my own wedding. But please do me one big favor and don't worry about me. This is your big day. You know that I will be fine. God will help me through this. And know that I am extremely happy for you and Roger."

"All right, Clarice. But if you need to talk please don't hesitate."

"Thank you Annette."

Oh Lord, Clarice prayed, *thank you for my wonderful friends. Even on their wedding day they would make time for me. I am forever grateful for their friendship. Lord, please help me to get through this. I don't want to take away from their joy. Please bless them abundantly, oh Lord.*

Clarice wiped away the tears that had rolled down her cheeks. She stuffed down her sad feelings and joined her friends with the resolution to enjoy this time of happiness.

The celebration lasted until after eleven o'clock. It was a clear night with a bright moon and sparkling stars. Roger and Annette said their goodbyes and left for their honeymoon.

"You should go home, Clarice," Lydia said. "You look tired."

"But we need to clean up."

"Why don't we meet up tomorrow morning? We can get everything done before and after the service."

"All right. The girls must be exhausted, too."

"I'm not tired," Isabelle said between yawns.

"Me neither," Lisa rubbed her eyes.

Lydia couldn't hide her amusement. "See you all in church tomorrow."

"Will seven be okay?" Clarice asked.

"Make it seven thirty."

"See you then Lydia."

Clarice sank into her bed after tucking Lisa and Isabelle in. Deep sadness overcame her. *Lord, I miss Quinn more than ever. Bless him and let him find You. May he make You Lord of his life. I want to see him finding peace and joy in You.*

With those thoughts she fell asleep.

Chapter Thirty-one

Lydia opened the door of the meeting room for Clarice with a cup of coffee in her hand. "I thought you might need some. There is more in the kitchen."

Clarice accepted the cup and sank onto a chair. "Oh Lydia, my heart almost bursts with all the pain I'm feeling. My marriage is broken beyond repair, I don't know where Norbert is, and I miss Fiona. I can't stand it anymore."

"God never gives us more than we can handle. Be strong Clarice. He is with you."

"I know, Lydia, but the pain inside feels so raw. I know that I need to trust God, but it just hurts so very, very bad."

"I expected you to feel a lot of pain, especially after watching Annette and Roger getting married yesterday."

"I am truly happy for them. They are very dear to me. But I had to think about my own wedding and my own vows. I never expected for my marriage to break. I feel like crying. But most of the time I have to control my tears and then when I'm alone the tears won't come. It feels like a deep sea of tears inside my heart. And I'm afraid that there will be a day when I can't control them anymore."

"Don't worry about that. Even your tears are in His control. And when they come they will be for God's glory somehow. Oh Clarice, God cares so much about you. He wants you to trust Him in every area of your life. Don't give up. He is preparing you for something big. Keep your eyes on Jesus."

"Thanks for your encouragement, Lydia. I feel a little better. Lately I've been very overwhelmed. But when I look to Jesus, I feel peace. I know that He sees the whole picture. I want to trust Him with all my heart."

"The verse comes to mind, *Trust in the Lord with all your heart and lean not on your own understanding. In all your ways acknowledge Him and He will direct your path.* Try to meditate on this verse today. God will encourage you to go on."

"Thanks. I appreciate your kind words. I guess we'd better get started if I want to have enough time to pick up the girls before the service."

"Okay. Then let's go."

They worked together and had everything except the vacuuming done before Clarice had to leave. "I'll see you in a few minutes," Clarice said and hurried to the car. The girls were ready and waiting for Clarice. They made it just in time before church started. After the service Clarice asked the girls to help with the vacuuming and they were done in no time. "Let's go to the park for a picnic," Clarice suggested.

"Oh, yeah. We haven't done that in a long time. Can we have rolls and bananas and chocolate milk and chocolate chip cookies?" they asked Clarice.

"Yes, why not. Let's go."

The afternoon was relaxing and fun filled. By evening everyone was tired and went to bed happy.

Chapter Thirty-two

Clarice woke up early Monday morning. The house was silent and the girls were fast asleep. *Thank you for waking me*, Clarice prayed. *I enjoy this quiet time with You. You are so good to me. I can trust You, even in this difficult time. You are in charge of my broken marriage. You watch over Fiona overseas. You know where Norbert is and You watch over him. Please keep him safe. My heart hurts very deeply, but in that hurt I feel Your comforting love. Thank you, Lord!*

Clarice lay awake another moment before sleep claimed her again. She woke up to Lisa and Isabelle arguing.

"I told you to wake me early, Lisa," Isabelle complained. "Why didn't you do it? Now I won't be able to finish my letter before we have to go to school."

"I tried to wake you five times. But you wouldn't wake up." Lisa protested.

"Of course it is my fault!" Isabelle exclaimed.

"It's definitely yours. I tried my best. But you just won't ever wake up." Lisa said with frustration.

Clarice stuck her head into their room. "Hey there, what's going on?"

"Lisa didn't wake me in time. Now I can't finish my letter before school."

"Mom, I tried waking her but she wouldn't get up."

"Hmm, sleepyhead. We will have to talk about it after school. Get ready, so we won't be late."

Clarice went back to the kitchen. *How can I get Isabelle to take responsibility for herself? Why is it so hard for her to see when she is wrong? Oh Lord, give me wisdom to deal with this.*

Lisa and Isabelle stormed into the kitchen with their backpacks. "I'm hungry, Mom," Lisa said.

"I'm starving," Isabelle chimed in.

One look at the girls made Clarice laugh. "Lisa, go back and brush your hair and Isabelle change that shirt. It's from yesterday and decorated with spaghetti sauce from dinner. A brush to your hair would also be nice. Oh, and don't forget about those teeth."

"But Mom, we're late," the girls protested.

"Just hurry," Clarice said, pointing to the door.

When the girls came back, Clarice could tell that they still rushed through their morning routine, but at least they looked somewhat acceptable. She handed each a granola bar and they rushed to the car. They arrived at the school just in time.

"Have a great day. I love you both."

"Love you too," they chimed and walked to their classrooms. Another hectic day.

Chapter Thirty-three

Clarice missed Fiona very much and relished every letter she received. Now the day of her return was finally here. Clarice went to the airport with Lisa and Isabelle and waited at the gate.

"Mom, I need to go to the restroom," Isabelle said.

"Do you know where it is?" Clarice asked.

"Yes, Mom. It is over there," she pointed to a sign they had passed on their way to the gate.

"Okay. Lisa, go with Isabelle and stay together you two."

"Do I have to go?" Lisa asked.

"Yes. There is safety in numbers," Clarice smiled at Lisa.

"But I don't want to miss Fiona's arrival."

"We'll wait here if she comes before you are back."

"Hurry," Lisa told Isabelle as they walked off.

Clarice turned her attention to the gate again. Fiona was already in sight. She came through the gate and Clarice embraced her. "I missed you so much."

"I missed you, too," Fiona said as she hugged Clarice back. "Where are Lisa and Isabelle?"

"They just went to the restroom and should be back any moment."

"There she is," Lisa yelled and ran into Fiona's arms. "I missed you."

Isabelle flung herself into Fiona's arms. "You're here, you're finally here."

"You two have grown. Let me look at you."

"I fit into your clothes now," Lisa said wearing one of Fiona's former dresses.

"It looks pretty on you."

"Did you know that Uncle Roger and Annette are having a baby?" Isabelle asked.

"Yes, Mom wrote and told me in a letter."

"It will be born very soon!" Lisa exclaimed.

They made their way to pick up the luggage. "Dad wanted to come to the airport too, but didn't get off work," Clarice said. "He will pick you up after dinner tonight for dessert."

"That sounds fine, as long as I can take a nap this afternoon."

"But we wanted to play a game with you," Isabelle complained.

"It will have to wait. I am very tired from the trip."

They picked up the luggage and went home. "I made your favorite stew," Clarice said.

"Thanks, Mom." Fiona sat down at the table. "I am hungry. The food on the plane wasn't exactly filling."

They ate and Fiona lay down for a nap. She fell asleep within minutes. Quinn picked her up as planned after dinner and took her for dessert.

Clarice smiled to herself. *Lord You brought my girl back home. You will bring back Norbert in due time. And I believe that You will heal my marriage too. Help me to trust You.*

Chapter Thirty-four

Clarice filled the last serving bowl and put it into the oven to keep it warm. "Are you done setting the table?" she asked the girls.

"Yes, Mom. Can we eat now?"

"No, you will have to wait until Uncle Roger and Annette are here."

"I see their car," Isabelle chimed and ran to the door. Lisa got there first and opened it wide.

"Hey there, you two. How are you?" Roger asked as he made his way to the door.

"Where is Annette?" they asked.

"She couldn't come. But she wants me to give you a hug and a kiss from her." He embraced the girls and placed a kiss on their foreheads. "My, it smells wonderful in here."

"Hi, Roger. Where is Annette?" Clarice asked as he stepped into the kitchen.

"She is home. The doctor put her on bed rest today. She had some bleeding."

"I'm sorry to hear that."

"Thanks. I originally wanted to cancel for tonight but Annette's friend Anna showed up for a visit. Anna promised to take care of Annette until I come home. They practically shooed me out of the house."

"Did the doctor say why she is bleeding?"

"He thinks that Annette works too hard. She has been busy cleaning everything, and I mean everything. She wouldn't stop even though she was exhausted."

"Sounds like the baby will be here very soon," Clarice said with a twinkle in her eye.

"I wish she would rest up a little more. She'll need the energy when the baby is born. So the prescribed bed rest came just in time."

"Don't worry so much, Roger. She'll be fine. Please grab the meat platter from the oven. And you, Lisa, go get Fiona. Isabelle, bring the water."

They all sat down. "Would you say grace?" Clarice asked Roger.

"Sure. Dear Lord, thank you for this wonderful meal. And thank you for our friendship. Be also with Annette and protect her and the baby. In Jesus' name. Amen."

Isabelle reached for the dumplings.

"Guests first," Clarice interrupted her.

"But Mom, this is my most favorite food in all the world."

"You can still mind your manners."

"All right then," Isabelle let go of the serving spoon reluctantly.

Roger filled his plate and waited for everyone to serve themselves. Then he started eating. "So, how is school going?" he asked the girls.

"Fine," they said.

"Is anything important going on in school?"

"No," they replied.

"You won't have much of a conversation with them tonight. When I cook this meal they just eat."

"I can understand that, it is tasty."

"Is the baby's room ready yet?" Clarice asked between bites.

"Yes. I put the crib together yesterday. Now the only thing missing is the baby," he smiled.

"I can't wait to see her," Clarice said.

"You mean him," Roger corrected.

"Did Annette have another ultra sound?"

"No, but I am sure the baby is a boy. And his name will be John."

"I was also sure Lisa would be a boy, blond with blue eyes."

"Well, if I am wrong it will be a Johanna instead of a John," Roger laughed.

"Mom, my stomach hurts," Lisa said.

"What's wrong?"

"I ate too much."

Roger smiled. "That's easy to do with such food. It tasted wonderful, Clarice," Roger said as he put down his napkin.

"I helped," Isabelle beamed.

"Me too," Lisa smiled.

"You ladies are awesome cooks," Roger complimented.

"We learned from the best," Fiona boasted.

"Of course," Clarice winked at Roger. "Please go get the pie, Fiona. And you two clear the table."

"If it has to be," Isabelle sighed.

"Don't make such a drama about it," Fiona said.

The pie was served and consumed in record time. "This pie is delicious," Roger smiled. "May I take a piece for Annette?"

"Of course. I will also fix her a dinner plate. She loves this dish a lot. If I had known she were on bed rest, I would have made time to see her. Tell Annette I'll come by tomorrow."

"She will be delighted to see you."

"Uncle Roger, can you read us a story before we go to bed?" Lisa asked, her favorite fairy tale book in her hand.

"Yes, I can."

"First get ready for bed, you two," Clarice urged.

"Mom, I'm leaving now. Lori just drove up." Fiona said.

"Okay. Be safe and come home right after the movie."

"Okay. Bye, Mom. Bye, Uncle Roger."

"Fiona has matured a lot. Soon it will be a boyfriend picking her up," Roger teased.

Clarice rolled her eyes: "I'm not ready for that. She was gone for so long and it is nice to have her back. I'm not ready for a guy to snatch her out of my hands yet."

Roger just smiled.

Lisa stormed into the room, Isabelle right behind her. "We are ready." They jumped onto the sofa to sit with Roger. Roger pulled them close and started reading. Clarice leaned back on the other sofa and closed her eyes. Quinn used to read to the girls. Oh Lord, why can't everything be okay? Tears threatened to fall and Clarice blinked them back.

"Will you sing for us?" the girls asked when the story was over.

"Of course. Please excuse me, Roger. I'll be right back."

Roger was reading the newspaper when Clarice returned. He looked up and put it aside. "Are you all right?" he asked.

"Don't ask. I will probably cry."

"You may use my handkerchief. Honestly, what's going on?"

"Oh, Roger. I'm hurting really bad. Quinn and I went to counseling together on Friday. I was hopeful that it would help us. Instead it felt like being stabbed in my heart over and over and over again."

"Why?" Roger asked as he joined Clarice on the sofa.

"Quinn says I need to earn his respect. He says I'm not an adult because I can't fully support the girls and myself. He said I broke my marriage vows because I changed. He attacked my faith and said that I don't have real faith. He also said that I am a liar. Oh Roger, what's the point to hold on to this marriage?"

Clarice sobbed as Roger held her close. "I want to get out of this marriage but I feel like God doesn't want me to give up. I don't see any hope for us. If Quinn sees me as that horrible person then what's the point of staying married? I don't understand why God wants to keep me in this relationship. Quinn weighs everything with money and by his standards. I don't know if I can stand it much longer. Is there anything I need to do for God to move and heal the marriage and my children? If so, I want to know what, because I have almost no tenderness left for Quinn. I can't handle this much longer."

Roger felt Clarice's agony and prayed silently. When Clarice finally calmed down he squeezed her hand gently. "I don't know what to tell you, except that I know that Jesus loves you and that He will see you through this."

"Thank you. I know. Please promise to pray for me, Roger. I can't take it anymore."

"Annette and I will pray for you every day. We actually pray for all of you already. Hang in there Clarice. You know that all things work for the good to them that love God and are called according to His purpose."

"I know. Thank you."

"I need to go back home. Annette is waiting. Thanks again for dinner."

"You're welcome. Thanks for coming. Hug Annette for me. I can't wait to see her tomorrow."

Clarice straightened the house a little. Dishes would have to wait till tomorrow. She was way too tired now.

Ten minutes later Fiona walked in the door. "Mom the movie was great. The main character Tony was absolutely dreamy. You have to see it too."

"Maybe the two of us can go to watch it when it comes out at the Dollar Movies?"

"That sounds great. I've got to go to bed now. Tomorrow I have a math test. Good night, Mom," Fiona said as she hugged Clarice.

"Good night, Fiona. Sweet dreams," Clarice hugged her back.

Clarice checked all the doors, turned off the lights and went to bed. *God, I need You. Help me. I feel worn out…* Clarice prayed as she drifted off.

I love you my child, I love you!

Chapter Thirty-five

Clarice rang the doorbell. "Come on in," Annette said as she opened the door. "How nice to see you. Roger told me that you would stop by today."

"I would have come yesterday, if I had known that the doctor had put you on bed rest. Sorry that you had to get up to answer the door."

"That's fine," Annette grinned. "I try to find excuses to move around. Lying in bed is unbearable when there is still so much to do."

"I thought Roger said that the baby room is completely finished. What else is left to do?"

"I need to wash out the cabinet, hang the curtains, scrub the bath tub, and a few other things."

Clarice laughed. "In your condition you won't be able to reach into the cabinets and it would be pretty amusing to see you scrubbing the bathtub with that large belly in the way!"

Annette looked at Clarice in disbelief. "Are you making fun of me?" she finally asked as she joined Clarice's laughter. Annette held her stomach as she tried to calm down. "If I go into labor today, it will be on your account. So what's new with you and the family?" Annette asked as they sat down on the sofa.

"Everything is going along as usual. I still don't know where Norbert is, but an old friend told me she saw him and he seemed to be okay. Unfortunately she didn't know anything else. I wish I could get in contact with Norbert. But knowing he is alive is better than nothing."

"That's true. And it is nice to know that God is watching over him."

"Yes, I am thankful for that."

"Have you noticed anything different about this room?" Annette asked with anticipation in her eyes.

"Not really," Clarice said as she looked around. Her gaze caught on a painting on the other side of the room. "Oh, my. You hung up my painting in your living room!"

"We finally found the perfect spot for it. Have you done any more work lately?"

"Actually, yes. I felt inspired to paint a lamb. It is almost finished."

"You have to show it to me, when you are done with it."

"I will. Annette, I have something encouraging to share with you."

"Go ahead. I am all ears."

"This morning I had a vision in my quiet time. God told me that He is in the process of healing Quinn's heart. I saw Quinn's heart in the Father's left hand and saw how He gently cleansed the wounds with great care and tenderness. Then God poured the healing balm of the Holy Spirit over Quinn's heart. God also told me that He will heal my marriage and my family."

"Oh, Clarice," Annette said with great joy. "I am excited for you. I always believed that God would heal your marriage. I can't express my joy about the news."

"I can't contain my own happiness too. Sometimes I get discouraged and want to give up. And I still don't see how my marriage and my family will be restored and healed. But knowing that the One in charge is the Lord God Almighty makes me very hopeful."

"Who knows, maybe it is just around the corner."

"I have been waiting for so long and can hardly wait for God to move. Quinn is still the only man I desire. I want to be embraced in his arms again."

"Let's wait in faith for God's perfect timing."

"As usual, I have to wait. That seems to be the story of my life."

"But at least you know who is working on your behalf while you wait."

"That's true. And I trust His timing."

"Thank you, Clarice, for sharing this good news with me. I am praying for you and Quinn and for your whole family. You all mean so much to me."

"You mean very much to me too. And seeing you and Roger so happy together is an extra blessing for me. After all you both are my dearest friends."

Annette rubbed her stomach. "Roger thinks that the baby will be a boy."

"What do you think, Annette?"

"I have to admit that I have no idea at all."

"Regardless if it is a boy or girl, I can see it already in my imagination. It probably has your beautiful hair with his gorgeous eyes."

"We'll see," Annette said. "I…" Annette held her stomach and breathed heavily.

"Are you all right?"

"I don't know. I just started hurting. But it is over already."

"I think you might be in labor. When is your due date?"

"The doctor says in a month." Annette had another contraction.

"I'll call Roger. He should take you to the hospital." Clarice dialed Roger's number. "Hey, Roger, it's Clarice. You may want to come and take Annette to the hospital. I think she is in labor. I am at your house and will wait till you are here."

"I'll be there right away."

"Do you have your hospital bag packed?"

"No. I was going to do it today."

"I'll help you. Which nightgown did you want to take?"

"The light blue in the first drawer."

"Rest up. I'll gather what you need."

"Thanks, Clarice."

Clarice put the last item into the bag when she heard the door. Roger dashed into the living room. "Annette, are you okay?"

"Yes. But the pain is coming every five minutes."

Clarice handed Roger the bag. "You should go now. Let me know when the baby is born."

"We will."

They all left the house and Clarice went home. *Be with Annette, oh Lord, and help her with the birth. Thank you that I was able to be there when she needed me. Give Roger the strength to watch Annette going through labor and delivery. Thank you that we can trust You in everything.*

Chapter Thirty-six

Clarice went home to prepare the kids' snacks for after school. *It really helps that Lisa and Isabelle can walk home by themselves now so that I don't have to drive to school all the time,* Clarice thought to herself. It freed her to get things done that she usually couldn't find time for. *I wonder when the baby will be born?*

Lisa and Isabelle came home and sat down with their snacks. "Annette is in the hospital and will probably have her baby today," Clarice informed the girls.

"Can we go and see it?" Isabelle asked with excitement.

"It is not born yet and unfortunately children are not allowed in the Baby Unit."

"That's not fair," Lisa complained.

"No reason to pout. Annette should be home a day after the baby is born anyway. I bet Annette and Uncle Roger will let us come by for a few minutes, to welcome the baby."

The phone rang. Clarice picked it up. "Hello," she said.

"Hi, it's Roger. The baby has been born. We have a little Johanna now. She is beautiful."

"So the little boy turned out to be a girl," Clarice said with a smug grin. "How is Annette doing?"

"Yeah. It's a girl, it's a girl," Lisa and Isabelle sing sang.

"Not so loud," Clarice told them.

"Annette is fine," Roger said. "I am so proud of her. She has given me one of the prettiest gifts ever. Little Johanna is so special."

"Tell Annette 'hi' from us and 'congratulations'. I should let you go to be with your girls again. Thanks for calling me!"

"You are welcome. I'll talk to you later."

The evening was spent with joy and excitement and Clarice could hardly get the girls to calm down. "Annette had a baby girl," they told Fiona when she came home.

"We better make them a card," she suggested and pulled out construction paper. It was bed time when they finished their creation.

Thank you, Lord, for blessing my dear friends with a beautiful girl. Be with them and watch over them, Clarice prayed when she finally lay in bed that night.

Chapter Thirty-seven

Lisa and Isabelle had just left the house to go to school when the phone rang. "Hi Clarice, it's Roger."

"How is the new Daddy doing?" Clarice said warmly.

"I am well. We will be discharged from the hospital today. I am a little nervous about bringing this beautiful, tiny baby home."

"You will be fine," Clarice assured Roger. "God will give you all the wisdom you need to care for Johanna."

"I know that I can trust God with this, it's just so new to me."

"Just give it some time. How is Annette doing?"

"She is fine. She is such a trooper. The way she holds and cares for Johanna astonishes me. It's as if the baby is part of her very self."

"Well it is. She has been carrying the baby for quite some time, if I may remind you," Clarice said with humor in her voice.

"Clarice, I feel so blessed. This is almost too much joy to contain."

"God is good. He blesses those who love him."

"Very true. Clarice, I want you to see this beautiful baby. Can you come by for a little while when we get home?"

"I would love to. The girls and I can't wait to see Johanna. Why don't you call me when you get home and settled in a bit?"

"I'll do that."

"Would it be okay if I bring the girls?"

"Of course. Johanna needs to meet her future baby sitters."

Clarice laughed. "You better believe it. Lisa and Isabelle practiced changing diapers on their dolls when they heard that the baby had been born."

Roger joined Clarice's laughter. "I'll be in touch."

"See you later and tell Annette hi."

Clarice sat down at the kitchen table and prayed. *Thank you, oh Lord, for blessing my wonderful friends with a beautiful baby. I know how much that means. You have blessed me four times and I thank you for each one of them.* Clarice took some time to pray for all of her children before she continued with her household chores.

Time passed quickly. Clarice was preparing dinner when Lisa and Isabelle came home from school. "How was school?" she asked them.

"Okay," they responded.

"Do you have homework?"

"I have just a little math," Lisa said.

"And I have to memorize a poem," Isabelle sighed while eating a cookie.

"Uncle Roger called. He said they will come home with the baby today."

"Can we go and see the baby?" the girls asked excitedly.

"Yes. But only for a short time. Annette still needs a lot of rest."

"When can we go?" Isabelle wanted to know.

"Uncle Roger will call me when they are ready for us. Let's get homework done quickly so we can leave right when he calls."

Both girls hurried to the task and were done in no time at all. "We are ready, can we go now?"

"Uncle Roger hasn't called yet. You can help wrap these outfits for the baby."

The phone rang. Isabelle ran to answer it. It was Roger. "Can we come now?" Isabelle asked while jumping up and down.

"Yes. We will be waiting for you."

"Mom, Mom, let's go. They are waiting for us."

Clarice wrapped the presents quickly and they were on their way.

"Mom she is beautiful," Lisa said when she saw Johanna.

"Let me see her, too," Isabelle said, squeezing between Lisa and Clarice.

"Oh, Annette. I am so happy for you," Clarice said with tears in her eyes. "May I hold her?"

"Of course," Annette said with a radiant smile.

"Congratulations again to you two. She is beautiful."

Roger smiled proudly. "Thanks."

They kept the visit short, so that Annette and Roger could get some rest. *Thank you, Lord, thank you,* Clarice prayed in her heart.

Chapter Thirty-eight

The phone rang. Clarice picked it up. "Hello."

"Hi, Clarice. It's Maeve. Do you think you could meet with me? I really need to talk to you."

"That's fine. Let's meet at Guiseppe's. I can meet you there in half an hour."

"Sounds good. See you then."

Maeve was late. Clarice ordered two salads for them knowing that her friend loved salad as much as she did. *Why did she want to talk to me so urgently*, Clarice thought. Maeve had become a Christian several years ago after joining Clarice for a church service. Clarice had mentored her ever since and they had formed a friendship.

Maeve entered the restaurant. "How are you, Clarice?" she asked.

"Fine. How about yourself?"

"I am well. Did you order yet."

"Yes," Clarice said as the waiter brought the salads and glasses of water. "So what's up?"

"I have had this on my mind for a while, and I believe it can't wait any longer."

"All right then."

"Clarice, I don't understand why you don't move on with your life. You should find a new partner. There is Peter, for example. He has come to our church for a whole year now. You could be very happy with him. And best of all he loves the Lord with all his heart."

"I know his devotion to God. That's the very thing that stands out about him."

"Then why don't you move on with your life? I know for a fact that he is attracted to you. The way he looks at you gives it away."

"Really? But he knows that I am married and therefore out of his reach," Clarice countered.

"Clarice, he also knows that your marriage is beyond repair. You have to move on with your life. There is simply no hope for the restoration of your marriage. It simply can't be fixed."

Tears ran down Clarice's cheeks. "I know that it seems impossible for my marriage to be restored. The most basic foundation is missing: trust. That's why I never agreed to let Quinn move back in again. I can't live with someone who without blinking an eye can lie to me."

"Clarice, you have to move on. I want you to have a happy marriage and I know that Peter would make you very happy. I am concerned that he could find somebody else. You have to leave the old marriage behind. It can't be fixed."

"I can't do that. I know that neither I nor any other person can fix my marriage. But I know that God can do what no human can. This is why I hold on to my marriage. I know that God is able to heal this mess. Deep down in my heart I have the assurance that He wants to restore my marriage and my family."

"But Clarice, God can't change Quinn's heart."

"This may sound silly, but I believe He can. In the Old Testament God hardened Pharaoh's heart toward Moses and the Israelites."

"He hardened it. He didn't soften it."

"That's true but in Psalms it also speaks about the fact that God is the One who forms the hearts of men."

"But that still doesn't change the fact that Quinn lies a lot. It is a choice to be deceptive."

"God can change even this. I truly believe that when Quinn gives his life to Christ he will change. I remind God of Saul who became Paul. I pray for a 'Road to Damascus' experience for Quinn."

"Let me be very honest, Clarice. I think you set yourself up for disappointment. I really believe it is time to set your wishful thinking aside and go on with your life."

"I know this all sounds weird, but I can't give up. I asked God to take that glimmer of hope away if He has different plans for my life. Instead of losing hope, I feel stronger than ever that God will heal my marriage."

"I still think you set yourself up for great heartache. Look at the facts Clarice: You've been separated for four long years now. You've struggled through financial hardship, you are lonely, and you don't have security. Peter would be an answer to all these areas. He makes good money and would be a good provider for you and the kids. You wouldn't be lonely anymore and could finally feel secure. Please open your eyes, Clarice. I am tired of seeing you suffer."

"This all sounds tempting but I need to hold on to God and I choose to believe in His healing power. Unless God shows me differently, I will hold on to my marriage."

"Forgive me for saying so, but you are hopeless, Clarice."

"On the contrary, I am hopeful regardless of the circumstances. Thank you for caring about me in such a deep way. But be assured that God will show up in a mighty way."

"I'm afraid I disagree. I still can't see it your way but I wish you the very best."

"Thank you for your honest concern. Your friendship means a lot to me. Oh my, we have hardly touched our salads. It's a good thing that we didn't order anything hot. It would be cold by now."

"You're right. What are you and the girls doing this weekend?"

"I will have to help at work for a couple of hours. I don't like that work cuts into my weekend time with the kids."

"I am sorry that you have to go in to work. Do you want me to pick up the girls and take them to the library for a couple of hours?"

"That would be wonderful. Besides, they love to spend time with you. They are impressed by all your knowledge about history. Isabelle wouldn't stop talking about your trip to the historic museum."

Maeve laughed, "You have some very special girls. I enjoy them so much. I wish I had children of my own every time I am around yours."

"You are too kind. I'll tell the girls to be ready on Saturday at nine. I bet they'll be ready by eight."

"Good, than that's set. I need to go now. Give the girls a hug from me."

"I will. See you later."

Clarice finished her salad. *Am I really setting myself up for great heartache? I have seen You move mountains in my life. Lord, if this all is really wishful thinking and You want me to move on, than make it absolutely clear to me. You know that I want to follow Your lead.*

Chapter Thirty-nine

Clarice drove aimlessly throughout the city streets, but, as so often happened, she found herself in the parking lot of her church. She parked the car and stepped inside. Around this time of day nobody would be there. She sat down on a chair and couldn't hold her tears back any longer. Clarice felt so hopeless. *Oh Lord*, she sobbed. *I was sure You would perform a miracle in my marriage and now it is over. Oh Lord, I am hurting so deeply. But I know that You have good plans for me. I can hold on to Romans 8:28 and know that even this will produce a blessing in my life. Lord, I wanted to praise You even when the road gets hard. And now the only thing I can do is hurt. Lord help me, I plead with You. Right now I wish I had never been born. That's truly how I feel.*

Clarice felt a hand on her shoulder and was startled. "Oh, it's you Sam," she said. She had met him, the new assistant pastor, and his wife May last Sunday after the service. They formed an instant connection. "How long have you been here?"

"Long enough to know that you are hurting."

Clarice looked down at her folded hands, tears rolling down her cheeks. "It is over, Sam. Quinn has filed for divorce. I received the papers this morning."

"I am very sorry, Clarice. Would you like to come to the office to talk? May is here for lunch and brought some tea."

"Yes, I would like that."

"Hi, Clarice," May said when they entered the office. "Are you all right?"

"Not really. I just received divorce papers from Quinn."

"Oh, Clarice," May embraced her. "Sit down and have a cup of tea."

"Thank you," Clarice took the cup that Sam handed her. "I am totally shocked. I really believed that God was turning the situation around. And now there is a divorce after all."

"That must be very hard," May said. "But know that we are praying and don't forget that we are here for you if you need us."

"I appreciate your offer. Actually, I would be relieved if I didn't have to go alone to court."

"Don't worry, Clarice. One of us will go with you," Sam assured her.

"Thank you. I think I've got to go. School is over in half an hour and I have to pick up Lisa and Isabelle."

"Bye, Clarice, and hang in there," Sam said.

May hugged Clarice. "God will see you through."

"Thank you." Clarice went to her car and headed for the school. She appreciated Sam and May. It was a relief to know that she didn't have to go alone through the divorce proceedings.

Clarice arrived at the school just in time. Lisa and Isabelle made their way to the car. "Hi, Mommy," they chimed and placed a big kiss onto Clarice's cheek. The girls had a lot to share on their way home but Clarice's thoughts wandered back to the divorce papers. *Help me Lord. Help me to be strong for the children. They will need me now more than ever.*

"Why are you crying, Mom?" Isabelle asked.

"I have a bad headache," Clarice replied leaving out the cause of it.

"Can you take me to the store?" Isabelle asked.

"No, Honey, I really feel very bad."

"But I really wanted to buy some chocolate," Isabelle said disappointedly.

"Didn't you hear Mom?" Lisa scolded her younger sister. "She feels rotten." Lisa turned to Clarice. "Can we help you with something when we get home?" she asked.

"That's sweet of you Lisa, actually you could get dinner started. We'll have canned ravioli."

At home, Clarice lay down on the sofa and tried to relax.

"Why don't you go to your room?" Lisa asked. "It would be quieter in there."

"I'd rather stay here with you guys." Clarice responded. Being alone would be the worst right now. She would end up in a crying fit if she was by herself.

Oh Lord, Clarice prayed, *the pain is greater than I ever imagined. Will I ever stop hurting?* Clarice's head was pounding by now.

The front door opened and Fiona entered. "Mom," she called out with excitement, "Mom, Mom!"

Lisa hushed her. "Mom is on the sofa with a bad headache."

Fiona went to the sofa with concern in her eyes. "Are you okay? Do you want me to get you an aspirin?"

"No, Honey," Clarice managed as she sat up. "You sounded excited when you came in. What's up? I could use some good news."

"Mom, I made the dance team. Our first practice is tomorrow after school."

"I am proud of you, Fiona, and I can't wait to see your first dance performance," Clarice smiled weakly.

"I'll bring you some water," Fiona said as she went to the kitchen. She came back with a tall glass of water and two aspirin.

"Thank you, Fiona," Clarice said and swallowed the pills. "I'll rest up a few more minutes."

"Take your time," Fiona said. "I'll watch out for the girls."

"Thank you, Honey," Clarice said and drifted into sleep. Two hours later she woke up, her head feeling better, but the divorce papers were right back on her mind. *Help me Lord, help me,* she prayed as she got up to check on the girls. They were in the kitchen cleaning the dinner dishes.

"This is still dirty," Isabelle said and put a plate back into the soapy water.

"Can't you wait or put it on the side. You really annoy me," Lisa complained loudly.

"Keep it down," Fiona reprimanded them. "Mom is trying to rest, and your fighting won't help her headache."

Fiona put a cup into the cabinet and turned around. "Oh, Mom, did we wake you?" she asked.

"No, Fiona, and I actually feel better. I slept longer than I had planned. Thank you for taking care of dinner and clean up."

"We saved some ravioli for you," Isabelle said and pulled a plate from the refrigerator.

"I don't feel like eating right now. I'll have some ravioli later. Did you do your homework yet?"

"We started," Lisa said, "but I am not finished. I don't understand the math problems."

"I am done," Isabelle said proudly. "I had to write a poem about the sunshine. You have to read it." With that Isabelle ran to the den and came back with a paper. She handed the poem to Clarice.

"Why don't you go ahead and read it for us?" Clarice suggested.

"Okay," Isabelle said and read:

> *The sun is round and beautiful,*
> *I love her ever so.*
> *She shines and lightens up my life*
> *With her pretty glow.*
> *When I see the sunshine's light*
> *About the Lord I think.*
> *For the Son lights up my life*
> *To that my heart does cling.*

"Did you come up with this poem by yourself?" Clarice asked in disbelief.

"Yes, Mom. It just came to me. I didn't really have to think about it."

"This poem is very beautiful, Honey."

"Mom, can I borrow the car?" Fiona asked. "I have to buy a poster board for science."

"Yes you may. Could you please pick up some milk and eggs on the way?"

"I will. See you later."

"Bye, Honey." Clarice handed her the car keys. *Fiona has grown up so much since she went overseas*, Clarice thought to herself.

Clarice tried to help Lisa with her math homework, but couldn't concentrate. "I am sorry, Lisa. My brain doesn't work tonight. Ask your teacher tomorrow to explain the problems to you."

"Okay," Lisa sighed.

"Girls, I am very tired. We will go to bed early today."

"But Mom, we have another hour before bed time," Isabelle complained.

"I need you to go to bed. You may read in your room for an hour."

"That's not fair," Isabelle was angry.

"Go change and brush your teeth. I want you in bed in five minutes," Clarice said sternly.

Fiona walked into the house. "Where are Lisa and Isabelle?" she asked.

"I sent them to bed early. They can read in their rooms until bed time. I will turn in too. Don't stay up too late."

"I won't," Fiona promised.

When Clarice was finally in bed, tears overcame her. She cried silently into her pillow. *Oh Lord, it hurts so much. Please help me.* Clarice fell into a restless sleep.

Chapter Forty

Quinn sat at his desk. He was working on a file when Pete, his awkward coworker, approached him.

"Can I help you with anything?" Quinn inquired, hoping to get rid of him fast.

"Actually, I'm fine. But I wanted to ask if you'd like to join us for dinner tonight. My wife prepared food for an Army. She is the best cook in town and we'd like you to share this feast with us."

"I planned to go grocery shopping after work," Quinn lied. "My refrigerator is totally cleaned out except for some bread and mayonnaise."

"If that's all, you don't have to worry. As I said, my wife cooks an abundance of food and she won't let anybody leave the house without some of the delicious leftovers."

"You guys should have opened a restaurant."

"We seriously considered it. But I love my job and my wife enjoys staying home with the kids, teaching them all she knows about cooking and baking. She excels in both. You should come and see, or I should say come, taste and see."

Quinn considered the offer. A nice home cooked meal sounded good. *I could put up with him for the benefit and duration of a nice meal.* "Okay. I'm curious now. When should I be over and where do you live?"

"How about five-thirty? I'll write down my address."

"Five-thirty sounds fine. Please write down the main cross streets as well. Now that I know that a feast is awaiting, I don't want to miss it on account of getting lost."

"Here is my address. I drew a map on the back of the paper. You can't miss it."

"Thanks for the invitation."

"You're welcome. We are looking forward to seeing you."

A home cooked meal. Can't beat that. Haven't had one for quite some time, Quinn thought as he returned to his file.

The day went by quickly and Quinn was satisfied with the progress he had made. He left the office and bought some flowers and chocolates. Quinn arrived at the house five minutes early.

"Come on in," Pete said as he opened the door. "Dinner will be ready in about ten minutes."

"It smells wonderful, Pete. Thanks again for having me over."

"It's our pleasure. Let's wait in the living room. You can give the flowers and chocolates to my wife when she is finished. I stay out of Marie's way when she cooks. She moves so fast, she could run you over," Pete said with a grin.

The men sat down on the sofa. Right across from them hung a painting. "That's pretty art work," Quinn said.

"It is indeed. Marie bought it at a craft show."

"My wife, or soon ex-wife, said at some point that God had spoken to her and that He had given her the gift of painting. I believe in God, too. But having Him talk to you is absurd. There are stories in the Bible, where God spoke to people. But any decent person knows that these are only made up stories. Besides, she draws like a preschooler."

"Quinn, with all due respect. I believe that the Bible is true and that God spoke to people and still does in various forms. One of them audible."

"You don't want to tell me that you hear God's voice?"

"Actually, I do. But there are many ways God speaks to me. Sometimes He just nudges my heart."

This is getting weird, Quinn thought. *It's impolite to leave now. Besides I really want to eat. It smells so delicious. I guess I can put up with a crazy person for the duration of a meal. I wonder how his wife deals with all this craziness.*

"You told me you have children," Quinn said to divert the conversation.

"I do. They are playing in the back yard. I need to call them in, if you don't mind."

"No, go right ahead."

Pete went outside to call the children in for dinner. Quinn decided to take a closer look at the painting. It was indeed a nice piece. While he studied it, he saw the artist's name. Clarice L.

"Clarice L.? That must be a coincidence. Clarice couldn't have done this painting," he mumbled to himself. Before he could ponder the thought some more, a woman with apron stuck her head in the living room. "It's time to eat."

"You must be Marie."

"I am. And you must be Quinn. Thank you for coming."

"These are for you," Quinn said, handing her the flowers and chocolates.

"Thank you. These are beautiful. I'll put them in a vase."

The room filled with laughter when Pete and his children entered the house. "Go and wash up. We don't want to make mom wait after all her hard work in the kitchen."

"I helped her peel the potatoes," little Sophie said with pride.

"Then they will taste extra special," Pete said with a warm smile.

Hands and faces were washed in no time and they all sat down at the table.

"You can sit here, Mister," Alfred said as he showed Quinn to a chair between his father and himself.

"Pete, will you say the prayer please?" Marie asked her husband.

"Of course, Darling" They all joined hands and Pete began. "Dear heavenly Father, thank you for this beautiful day, our wonderful children and our honored guest. Bless the food and let it be nourishing to our bodies, that we may be filled with strength and may bring you Joy, Praise and Glory. We love you, Lord! In Jesus' name we pray. Amen."

The hand holding and prayer made Quinn uncomfortable. He wasn't used to any of this. After all there were special prayers known that you were supposed to say before you eat and not like this, informal and all. His thoughts shifted quickly when serving bowls and platters were passed to him. They all filled their plates with tender chicken cordon bleu, crisp mashed potato croquettes, steamed asparagus wrapped in bacon, cauliflower gratin topped with Dijon hollandaise and garlic roasted carrots.

"This is truly a feast," Quinn said between bites. "Everything tastes delicious."

"Thank you for the compliment," Marie beamed. "I'm glad you like it."

"Like it? I love it!"

"Make sure to keep some room for dessert," Pete warned.

"I'll try. But to be honest, I'm kind of getting full already."

"That's fine. We'll have some coffee after dinner and eat dessert a little later."

"Sounds like a plan," Quinn replied.

When everyone was done, they all moved to the living room.

"Daddy, can we do our Bible reading now?" little Ruthie asked.

"Would you mind, Quinn?"

"No that's fine." Even though he was opposed to all that Christian stuff, the sincere interest and excitement of little Ruthie warmed his heart.

Leslie, the ten-year-old, passed out Bibles to everyone. Quinn felt uncomfortable again.

"Let's go to Mark 10," Pete said opening his Bible.

Where can I find Mark 10? Quinn thought as he looked for a table of contents.

"Let me help you," Pete said, took Quinn's Bible and opened it to the tenth chapter of Mark.

"Let's start with verse 17."

"May I read?" Alfred asked.

"You may," Pete agreed.

"As Jesus started on his way, a man ran up to him and fell on his knees before him..."

Good grieve, Quinn thought to himself. *Why would anyone fall to his knees before Jesus? How can anyone belief that stuff? People are too gullible. I can't wait until we are finished with this nonsense.*

"Jesus looked at him and loved him..."

Jesus loved him. Yah right.

Quinn read along halfheartedly, when suddenly his heart began racing.

"Then come follow me..."

'Come follow me' almost jumped off the page at him. What was he to make of this. It was as if these words were directed at him. Tears were running down his cheeks as he muttered, "How could I follow You? You are God. You are pure and I can't approach You. Haven't You heard how I just mocked You in my thoughts? How I consistently mocked You throughout my life? I always gave Clarice a hard time for her faith. But it was You whom I fought, not her. No God, I am not worthy that You care for me."

Quinn felt Pete's arm on his shoulder. "God loves you, Quinn. He has great plans for you."

"But I don't deserve His love."

"None of us do. We all are sinners in dire need of a Savior. That's why Jesus died for us. He knew that we couldn't get right with God by ourselves."

"But why do I feel so dirty?"

"You don't have to feel that way anymore. If you ask Jesus to forgive your sins and give him the reigns of your life, He will cleanse you from all unrighteousness and lead you on a new path."

"So how do I do that?"

"You just have to ask him for forgiveness of your sins and give Him Lordship over your life."

"Do I have to go to my knees? And do I have to go to church for that?"

"No, Quinn. You can take care of it right where you are. God is here with us and wherever we go."

Quinn sobbed. "Oh, Lord God. Cleanse me from all my sins. Forgive me. I want to live my life for You. Take over my life. I need You so much."

Everyone had tears of joy in their eyes. "Mommy, is he now family, too?" little Sophie asked.

"Yes, he is, Honey."

Sophie went over to Quinn and gave him a big hug. "I am happy that you are family now."

"Me too," Quinn said with a tender smile.

"Can we have our dessert now?" Alfred asked with hopeful anticipation.

"Yes, we can. I'll bring it out right now," Marie said. "It is time to celebrate!" She came back with a tray of pistachio cream in dessert bowls topped with a dollop of whipped cream and garnished with chocolate shavings and a waffle heart.

"This is delicious," Quinn said after his first taste. "How do you stay so slim with all this wonderful food, Pete?"

"I guess I must have a high metabolism." Pete chuckled.

"Thanks again for having me over for this wonderful feast."

"You can thank God for being here. He spoke to my heart to invite you for quite some time. But I wasn't very confident to ask you. You have a reputation at the office of coming down on Christians pretty hard and I wanted to avoid you for that reason. But God kept nudging my heart until I finally surrendered. So, if you want to thank anyone, it should be the Lord."

Quinn smiled at Pete. "Thanks for obeying."

"You're welcome, Quinn."

The men talked for a few more hours. Finally, Quinn got ready to go. "We have to meet soon again. I have so many questions and would like to see what you have to say about them."

"We'll do that. I am glad that you are my brother in Christ now."

"Me too. Have a good night and see you in the office in the morning."

"Bye, Pete."

That night Quinn lay in bed reflecting on the events of the evening. *I am now also one of those crazy Christians,* he smiled to himself. *And I never felt better in my whole life.* "Thank you, Jesus, for Your love and for Your patience with me. I promise to follow You wherever You lead me." With those words he fell asleep.

Chapter Forty-one

Roger was about to get ready for lunch when he heard a knock at his open door.

"May I come in," Quinn asked.

"I am not sure if that's a good idea," Roger answered feeling anger welling up in him. Quinn had nerve showing up at his office after what he had done to Clarice.

"It is rather important," Quinn insisted.

"Okay, I'll give you five minutes."

"It's about Clarice."

"We'll take care of her."

"Please no! I mean that's nice of you. But I would like to do that myself."

"She needs someone who cares for her feelings, not someone who tramples them."

"I know," Quinn interrupted. "And I do care deeply for her feelings."

"You have a weird way of showing that. She cried for days."

"I can't say that I'm proud of anything I said to her when I handed her the divorce papers. But I want things to change."

"I can't follow you. Why don't you have a seat and explain it to me?"

"Thanks. A couple of days ago my co-worker invited me over for dinner. I accepted, even though he always seemed a little odd to me. He is one of those 'always happy' guys. When we sat down to eat he prayed over the food. I do that too before I eat but there was something totally different about his praying. I couldn't put my finger on it. Dinner was great even though they talked the whole time. I usually like dinners quiet but I enjoyed this meal tremendously. After dinner my coworker invited me to stay for devotions. I didn't really know what to expect but accepted anyway. Before I knew it, we all sat in the living room, each with a Bible in our hands. We read in Mark 10 about the Rich Young Man."

"I just read that with Annette the other day. But go on, I'm curious to hear what happened."

"While we read I got stuck on the last part of verse 21: *Then come, follow me.* I felt like Jesus was talking directly to me. I don't know what really happened but tears started streaming down my face. I knew in my heart that I wanted to follow Jesus. When my coworker and his family realized that I was crying they gathered around me and started praying over me. That night I accepted Christ as my Lord and Savior. It has changed my life."

"Quinn, I am so completely happy for you. Welcome to the family of believers. Did you tell Clarice yet?"

"Not yet. I drove by her house several times but didn't have the courage to go in. I want to grow old with Clarice by my side. But I don't know if she can forgive me for all I said to her when I handed her the divorce papers. I saw her break under the heavy accusations and harsh words that I threw at her, which I dare not repeat."

"It upset her greatly, Quinn. But I am sure she will forgive you. She always cared for you deeply, and I know that she always loved you."

"This time I might have killed whatever love was left. I feel terrible and hopeless."

"Quinn, I know Clarice very well. I am convinced that she has enough compassion in her heart to forgive you."

"But what if she is done for good with our marriage? I couldn't handle that."

"Quinn, I'll promise to pray for you. You need to go and talk to her. I encourage you to put it off no longer."

"I will try to talk to her this week," Quinn said. "Please do me a favor, Roger, and don't tell her any of what I told you."

"You have my word on it. I will only talk to God about it."

"Thanks, man. I don't remember being this nervous since I got married."

"Know that God is on your side no matter the outcome."

Quinn sighed, "I'll try to remember. Now I have taken up way too much of your time."

"That's okay. It's the least I can do for a new brother in Christ. God bless you, Quinn. Let me know how things go."

"I will. Thanks again." Quinn was about to leave, but turned around. "Roger, I have to ask you for another favor."

"What's that?"

"God has convicted me of the way I treated Clarice and the kids. I want things to work this time. Things have to change. I have to change. But I don't know how."

"Quinn, the most important step is to look to Jesus in everything. Accept His leadership over your life and ask Him to show and guide you in your leadership of your marriage and family. It might take some time. But God is faithful. And try to read as much as you can in your Bible. When God shows us something, He is also there to help us achieve it as we reach out to Him for help."

"Thanks, man."

"You're welcome. If you want to, you can join the Men's Group at our church. We meet once a week on Thursdays at six in the evening to grow in the Lord and to encourage each other."

"Thanks. I will try to come. See you later."

"Bye, Quinn."

After Quinn left, Roger knelt down. *"Thank you, Lord God, for Your faithfulness. Clarice has prayed so long for this to happen. Bless both of them and restore all the years that the enemy has stolen from them. I just want to praise You, oh Lord, my God."*

Chapter Forty-two

Clarice and Lydia sat down on the sofa. "Thank you for coming over, Lydia. I have to admit that I feel a little shaken. Tomorrow I will sign those papers, and it will be over."

"Clarice, I can't tell you how bad I feel for you."

"Thanks. At least I have some good news. Norbert made contact with me. He is in town."

"That is indeed good news. When are you going to see him?"

"I don't know yet. But at least I know he is safe. I can't tell you how much it hurt when I didn't know where he was and if I would ever see him again."

"I can only imagine what you went through."

"But let's not dwell on that. I am thankful to God that He watched over Norbert and brought him back into my life. God is more than able to turn things around. And as much as it hurts, I am ready to accept that God didn't heal my marriage."

"Clarice, I am thankful, that you kept your faith in God, even though He didn't bring healing to your marriage."

Tears ran down Clarice's cheeks. "I am hurting. There is no denying that fact. I was so sure that God had planned to reconcile us. But I can't turn away from God, just because He said no. I truly love the Lord. I know and pray, that nothing will ever separate me from Him. He is my very air I breathe."

"You don't know how much you bless me, Clarice. Going through all you've gone through and still holding on to your faith is a great witness."

"I can't say that I never questioned God, or why He didn't seem to show up at times. But the one thing I never had to question was His sincere concern for me. Lydia, in everything that happened in my life, I could feel God's loving presence. He allowed me to grow in my faith and gave me peace in the midst of the storms of life. He is my very rock in times of trouble. I truly love Him."

"Your life bears witness of your love for God."

"Thanks. Yours does too, Lydia."

"I have to go now. Stay strong, Clarice."

"I will try. God bless you."

Clarice closed the door behind Lydia and sat back down on the sofa. She picked up her Bible and tried to read. Tears welled up in her eyes. *Why can't my emotions line up with what I know about You? You have good plans for my life. There is hope in this hopeless situation. My future is in Your hands and I know that You love and carry me. I will trust in You and Your unfailing love.* Tears kept rolling down Clarice's cheeks. She didn't fight them anymore. In the midst of the pain she felt embraced by God's love.

The doorbell rang. Clarice wiped her face and answered the door. "Hi, Sam. How was the basketball game?"

"It was good. My team lost, but they played well."

"Would you care for some tea?"

"Yes, thanks."

Clarice filled two cups and sat down at the kitchen table.

Sam studied her face. "Tough morning?" he asked.

"Pretty much." Tears ran down her face. "I can't believe that the signing of the divorce papers is tomorrow. I believed this marriage could be saved and now it is over anyway."

"Has Quinn talked to you lately?"

"No. But I heard that Quinn accepted Jesus as his Lord and Savior. I hoped that this would change things. But Quinn hasn't come by at all."

"I'm sorry, Clarice."

"Thanks, Sam. Will you still be able to go with me tomorrow to sign the papers?"

"Yes, of course. Is there anything I can do for you? I'm off work today and tomorrow."

"Actually, yes. Could you check the kitchen sink for me? It is leaking again."

"No problem." Sam went right to it. "Do you still have some of the sealing strip?"

"Yes. It's in the closet with the tools."

The doorbell rang. "I'll answer this real quick. Let me know if you need my help."

Clarice opened the door. Color left her face when she saw Quinn. "May I come in?" he asked.

"Of course," Clarice managed to say. She closed the door behind Quinn.

"Clarice, the most wonderful thing happened to me. I found the Lord and life has new meaning to me. I feel such joy and peace. I wanted to come right away to share this good news with you. And I wanted to see if you would be willing to give our marriage another chance. I hurt you deeply with my words when I gave you the divorce papers, and I am very sorry. Can you forgive me, and will you give us another chance?"

Tears ran down Clarice's face. Before she could answer, Sam appeared in the doorway.

Quinn looked at Clarice. "I am sorry. I should have realized that you moved on with your life." Quinn turned around to leave.

"Wait," Clarice managed to say under tears. "Who said I moved on? Don't you realize I was waiting for this day? I have stood in prayer for us for so long. I know that I was often frustrated and not very kind. But I always hoped this day would come and our marriage would be healed."

Sam cleared his throat? "I better get going. Call if you need anything."

"Thanks, Sam. Please say hi to May."

"I thought Sam was…" Quinn stumbled.

"He is a very good friend who helped me with the divorce paperwork."

"So you mean it? You are willing to give us both another chance?"

"Yes, I do. Can you forgive me for all the hurt I caused you?"

"Only if you can forgive me. I didn't realize how insensitive I have been to you and the kids. I would do anything if I could turn back the clock."

"We can't change things from the past, but we can start over."

"Yes, and this time with our foundation in Christ. Oh Clarice, I love you so much," Quinn said and kissed her. "Do you have time to go with me for a little ride? I have a surprise for you."

"Yes I do. Just give me a moment to wash up."

Clarice washed her face and combed her hair. She changed into her favorite dress and took the time to find matching earrings and a necklace. A hint of mascara and lip gloss and she was ready to go. *Thank you, oh Lord my God, for answering my prayers. You always come through.*

Quinn was waiting in the living room praying and thanking God as well. He took Clarice into his arms again when she entered the room. "You are the most beautiful woman on this earth, inside and out." He kissed her again passionately. "We better go now. It is getting pretty hot here with you in my arms." He led her to the car and opened the passenger door.

Clarice climbed in and asked Quinn when he sat down beside her, "Where are we going?"

"You'll see."

They arrived at the mall and went inside.

"You must have read my mind. I'm starving."

"Actually, that's not why I brought you here." Quinn said as they came to stand in front of the jewelry store. "I want us to wear wedding rings again. Which one would you prefer?"

Clarice looked up at Quinn, tears rolling down her cheeks. She opened her purse and pulled out their wedding rings. "I would prefer these."

Quinn pulled Clarice into his arms. "You have our rings?"

"Yes. I have carried them for over a year now, hoping the day would come, when we would need them."

Quinn took one ring and carefully slid it onto Clarice's finger. "Until death do us part."

Clarice slid the other ring onto Quinn's finger. "Forever and always."

Quinn pulled her close and kissed her until she almost fainted.

Clarice realized people were looking at them. "We are not alone."

"I don't care," Quinn said and kissed her again.

About the author

Beate Keller was born in Frankfurt, Germany, grew up in Egelsbach, and moved to Albuquerque, New Mexico, after marrying Patrick. Together they have six children of whom five live in Albuquerque and one in Montana.

Beate works with children in a child care facility and writes in answer to a calling of God. She enjoys baking, cooking, singing, reading and spending time with her family and friends.

www.ingramcontent.com/pod-product-compliance
Lightning Source LLC
Chambersburg PA
CBHW030116100526
44591CB00009B/410